**This is what participants have s[aid about]
workshops o[n...]**

'I had never thought of using sad time[s...] inspiring and practical!'

'I will take away stillness: sitting with sa[dness...] and oneness: accepting where I'm at—it's okay and I don't need to feel guilty. I can move on when I am ready. Letting go of the guilt allows this movement.'

'It was really valuable to explore longing as a sense of being called towards something, rather than as craving or lack. I have struggled with this for years and I have a whole new way of looking at it now.'

'I will take away the understanding of not only allowing sadness, but actually giving it thought and meaning.'

'Exceptional, humble, wise. I am taking away a whole new way of relating to difficulty and struggle. What a relief!'

'I will go away with new and energised intention to make more meaning in the work I do.'

'Looking at how I create meaning in my life was very pertinent for me.'

'This material is very much needed in the world. I can see myself using this in my psychology practice on a daily basis.'

'The two days had a wonderful flow that led to a greater understanding of the role of sadness in my life.'

'I am taking away many creative ideas about how to incorporate these techniques into my work with clients and in my own life.'

'I have always known that there were valuable things to learn from sad times, but now, having learnt about the cycle of soulful melancholy, I know what to do to find them.'

'I am taking away a renewed sense of curiosity and gentleness about everything I experience.'

'I was intrigued and moved to learn more about the value and beauty of longing.'

THE USES OF SADNESS

WHY FEELING SAD IS NO REASON NOT TO BE HAPPY

KAREN MASMAN

First published in 2009

Copyright © Karen Masman 2009

All rights reserved. No part of this book may be reproduced or transmitted in any form or by any means, electronic or mechanical, including photocopying, recording or by any information storage and retrieval system, without prior permission in writing from the publisher. The Australian Copyright Act 1968 (the Act) allows a maximum of one chapter or 10 per cent of this book, whichever is the greater, to be photocopied by any educational institution for its educational purposes provided that the educational institution (or body that administers it) has given a remuneration notice to Copyright Agency Limited (CAL) under the Act.

Allen & Unwin
83 Alexander Street
Crows Nest NSW 2065
Australia
Phone: (61 2) 8425 0100
Fax: (61 2) 9906 2218
Email: info@allenandunwin.com
Web: www.allenandunwin.com

National Library of Australia
Cataloguing-in-Publication entry:

Masman, Karen.

    The uses of sadness: why feeling sad is no reason not to be happy / Karen Masman.

    978 1 74175 757 6 (pbk.)

    Sadness. Maturation (Psychology). Depression, Mental.

152.4

Internal design by Christine Schiedel, Chilli Creative Consultants
Set in 9/12pt Helvetica Neue by Midland Typesetters, Australia
Printed in Australia by McPherson's Printing Group

10 9 8 7 6 5 4 3 2 1

CONTENTS

Acknowledgements		VII
Introduction		1
CHAPTER ONE	When Sadness Comes Calling	5
CHAPTER TWO	Soulful Sadness	15
CHAPTER THREE	The Cycle of Soulful Sadness	27
CHAPTER FOUR	The Soul Calls—Longing	39
CHAPTER FIVE	Entering Liminal Space—Not Knowing	51
CHAPTER SIX	Attending to Stillness—Deep Listening	67
CHAPTER SEVEN	Encountering Grace—The Turning Point	83
CHAPTER EIGHT	Embracing Contradictions—Holding The Opposites	101
CHAPTER NINE	Befriending Yourself—Making Conscious Choices	117
CHAPTER TEN	The World Calls—Offering	133
CHAPTER ELEVEN	Go On With Your Story	147
Appendix		161
References and Further Reading		165

ACKNOWLEDGEMENTS

The fact that I am able to experience my life as fortunate and filled with happiness can be traced back to one piece of extraordinarily good fortune. At the age of 23 I met the meditation master Swami Muktananda, and his successor Gurumayi Chidvilasananda, and embarked on the path of Siddha Yoga. It is through this path that I am continuing to learn how to direct my attention inside and how to let my mind rest in my heart and awaken to the gifts of everything that arises in the crucible of everyday living—including sadness. I thank them for this with all my heart.

I would also like to thank the following people for their encouragement and contributions; their support is deeply appreciated: Jane Bennett, Michelle Clark, Linda Crawford, Shalini Davies, Suzanne Fizdale, Step Forbes, Rob Forbes, Sally Forbes, Marco Guzzi, Sandy Harman, John Holton, Gillian Hume, David Johnson, Tim Lane, Caitlyn Lehmann, Freya McIntosh, Karen Mallison, Judy Munro, Sharmila Nezovic, Allen Nixon, Kate Noonan, Colleen Noonan, Toni Pellas, Alexandra Pope, Imelda Samperi and Edweena Walker. I would also like to thank Russell Deal and the team at St Luke's Innovative Resources, where, as the managing editor and a workshop facilitator, I was able to trial some of the material for this book.

I would particularly like to acknowledge authors Thomas Moore and James Hillman for the important role they have played in bringing the word 'soulful' into my vocabulary and for sharing their deeply contemplated understandings of it through their writing.

I thank my publisher, Maggie Hamilton, and the team at Allen & Unwin in Sydney, especially Lauren Finger, Joanne Holliman Katri Hilden, Christine Schiedel and Kathy Mossop. The warmth of Maggie's welcome truly astonished me and I am very grateful for her luminous companionship every step of the way.

I thank the participants in my workshops and those friends and colleagues caught in random conversations, whose contributions have been pivotal for me in ways that have now become part of my being.

Most especially I thank my beloved family: my husband Kevin, and my children Nicholas, Alice and Louis. My love and gratitude also extends to my parents Nita and Rex, my sister Sue, my brother David, and their partners and children.

Thank you all.

INTRODUCTION

I would describe myself as a deeply happy person, so writing a book called *The Uses of Sadness* may seem like an odd thing to do. While being aware of living a truly fortunate life, I am drawn to the mystery of sadness. For me, learning to digest sadness is a fundamental part of learning the art of making happiness. Looking back through my toppling stacks of journals and notebooks I see that I have been exploring this gentle art of sublimation for many years.

I am grateful to say that the sadness I have experienced has not been the outcome of traumatic events, but rather the everyday challenges of living, loving, longing and letting go. And what a journey that is; there's more than enough difficulty—and joy—right there!

We humans are capable of experiencing great joy, and we are also visited by the sadness of difficulty and loss. Sadness may come right on cue or it may arrive when you least expect it. Whatever the circumstances, sadness is a much maligned emotion. As a society we do not deal with it well. Often our first response is fear and panic. We think it means something has gone wrong and our knee-jerk reaction is to mask it and try to get rid of it as soon as possible. We want people to move out of it quickly, especially young people; 'What's wrong?', 'Buck up!' or 'Snap out of it', we may say.

As a society we have a growing tendency to think that sadness is depression and this leads us to reach for a medical solution. While depression is a serious and widespread illness that deserves professional care, sadness is not depression. Sadness is a healthy and appropriate response to experiences of loss and disappointment, whether personal or global. In the face of the loss of species, or the prevalence of war and cruelty, why would we not feel sad? And deep within our being, as we face disappointment and shed ideas, relationships and dreams that no longer sustain us, sadness helps us gather the momentum for change. We can allow our times of sadness to deepen our connection with ourselves and others, and lead us to appropriate action.

Sadness can be a potent time for reflection, a call for down time and retreat, a sign of transition, a force for change in how we do things, a time for taking stock and discovering the sweet-tempered moments of being quiet and alone. Sadness can help us heed our soul's longing for greater wholeness and connection, it can deepen our capacity to listen, it can slow us down, soften our hard edges, teach us to let go, cause us to sharpen our intention and purpose, and help us to discover a world of beauty. It is a rich time for practising creativity and a sense of fearlessness. It is a time for honing our ability to notice the tiny moments of upliftment that are sparking throughout the day.

Sadness can be wistful, soft and sweet, or it can be hot and searing. It can shake us to our very foundations. However, in recoiling from our sadness too quickly we lose the opportunity to experience the gifts that sadness can bring. What if we decided to move closer to our sadness? What if we became curious about it? Rather than trying to fix it or banish it, what if we decided to remain present as it evolves within us, noticing how it subtly changes, and following its lead?

Our attention has great power. Under our steady and compassionate gaze things can transform. This is how an experience of sadness opens up and releases its gifts—through our generous attention, steady presence and sense of adventure.

I decided to watch sadness in this way. I asked myself: how do I know when it first arises; what happens next; how does it change; which activities are useful during sad times and which ones are not; and, very importantly, what is the point of sadness? As I closely observed sadness arising and subsiding, I noticed that there seemed to be a discernable pattern of seven phases. This book is based on that seven-phase cycle. The cycle is not a blueprint or a set of rules for getting sadness 'all neatly sorted'. On some level sadness always undoes us a little—that is part of its transformative power. However, the cycle can be used as a flexible map for travelling with awareness and creativity in the territory of sadness. Each of the seven phases (discussed in detail in Chapters Three to Ten) has a particular flavour and represents a doorway of opportunity for learning and enrichment.

By experimenting with the seven phases you will begin to penetrate the experience of sadness and gather skills in working creatively with it. Your sense of resilience will grow as you shed a little of the fear that can accompany sadness. You will discover unique ways of moving more fluidly through it and bringing what you learn into your life. Your deeper knowledge of the territory of sadness will also help you to recognise when you have become stuck and need help. These skills can be shared with others either professionally or in your own personal life.

The terrain of sadness is explored in a number of ways in this book. Firstly, through stories. Some of these are drawn from my own life and some come from the lives of others, including children. Some were gathered especially for this book, some emerged in workshops when the material was being developed, and some were drawn from the lives of well-known people. Except for the stories of famous people, all names have been changed.

You will find many suggestions for activities dotted throughout these pages. These simple, enjoyable and hopefully soulful activities can be used to explore the different phases of melancholy as the cycle unfolds. They include things such as sitting in a café or garden, finding objects, creating collages and maps, responding to questions, drawing and painting, listening to music, reflecting quietly, carrying things around in your pocket, body movements and—my particular favourite—lying on the floor and doing nothing. Many of the activities feature journaling and other creative writing techniques. Writing can be a very effective way to apply your creativity to your experience of sadness. It is a great tool for recording insights, noticing patterns, acknowledging and naming feelings, developing plans, telling stories, finding peace and equilibrium, recording and reflecting on quotes that intrigue you, and capturing snippets of dialogue and family events. It is a reflection tool, a contemplation tool and a study tool. Journal writing is a way of synthesising, clarifying, asking, imploring, noticing, making sense, coping, making meaning and digesting your experiences.

Journaling is effective because there can be healing and delight in simply naming and describing an experience, rather than needing to solve it. It is so satisfying to find exactly the right word or image for how you are feeling. Somehow the experience can settle inside when it finds a place to rest under its correct name. Not only is it healing to name an experience, it is healing to tap into your own creativity through the act of writing. Your notebook, exercise book, sheets of coloured paper, diary or journal can be your companion as you explore the seven phases of soulful sadness. As you are pondering, you can use your journal to distil your thoughts, to gain perspective and understanding, and to connect with what is deep inside. As you write, draw, paste or doodle in your journal you are like a dowser using a divining rod to locate an underground stream. Simply begin by jotting down words, thoughts and images without worrying about grammar, writing between the lines or being anything remotely resembling a 'good' writer. You can embellish the truth and even make up complete fabrications if you want. That can be a very creative and even hilarious way of uncovering what is there—even if it is sad.

There is a word that used to be part of the English language, and perhaps it is now time to reclaim it: 'unsoulclogged'. According to Jeffrey Kacirk, author of *The Word Museum*, it means 'not weighed down in spirit'. I hope that the seven-phase cycle of soulful sadness explored in this book will offer people ways of making peace with sadness as one of the many flavours of a rich life. I hope that the cycle will enhance our capacity to move through sad times towards engagement with our lives in ways that leave us feeling lighter, more joyful . . . and unsoulclogged! May we all come to know ever more deeply that feeling sad is no reason not to be happy.

CHAPTER 1
WHEN SADNESS COMES CALLING

CHAPTER ONE

Most of us are not that good at dealing with sadness even though we experience it on a regular basis. When sadness comes calling, we don't find it a comfy seat, and we don't listen to it carefully or converse with it creatively. We're likely to jump in and finish its sentences with all the same old things we've been saying for years. We're even more likely to ignore it or, increasingly, to spike its drink so we don't have to feel anything at all. Really, we simply want our sadness to go away, to disappear so it won't bother us. Because of this we have no idea of the rich gifts it offers us.

The reality is, we all feel sad sometimes. Sadness visits us in all kinds of hues—mildly blue, gut-wrenchingly black and shadowed, bruised purple, uniformly grey, or vaguely existentially beige. There are many reasons for feeling sad—obvious reasons, mysterious reasons, bizarre reasons—or no discernable cause at all. Sometimes we feel sad at moments when we think we shouldn't, such as at Christmas or at a birth or a wedding. Then we may even feel sad about being sad!

Sometimes sadness creeps up slowly as it can with the midlife blues, or it may come on suddenly and inexplicably while we are mid sentence or at the quiet end of a long day. At other times it may come calling right on cue, such as at retirements and farewells. Whatever the conditions that give rise to our feelings of sadness, one thing is certain: sadness is part of our experience of being human.

So why do we make it so wrong and why are we so afraid of it?

NO SADNESS ALLOWED—JULIE

In my family we were not allowed to be sad. We had to pretend that everything was always going really well. It was a matter of family pride. Actually, in our family being sad was seen as self-indulgent and weak. It really was a case of 'stiff upper lip' and 'soldier on'. I only found out years later that Mum was on and off antidepressants for most of my childhood. I had the feeling that something was wrong but I could never quite put my finger on it. I thought there was probably something wrong with me. I managed to ignore that nagging feeling for a long time by trying really hard to do everything right. Then as a middle-aged adult I went through a long time of being just so angry. I felt furious nearly all the time. I turned into the dragon lady from hell. The smallest thing could trigger me off. When everything finally fell apart and I was forced to stop and face my life, I discovered that underneath a lot of that anger was a little girl who was sad. It was so hard, but that was the beginning of a lot of positive change for me.

What if we brought a lot more attention to our experience of sadness? What if sadness contained gifts that could deeply enrich our lives? What if we became very skilled at extracting the juice out of our moments of sadness? What if in bringing our careful attention to sadness, in turning our clear and unblinking gaze on it, we were able to watch it transform before our eyes and yield its treasures? And here's a truly radical thought: what if we learnt the knack of making happiness out of sadness?

In thinking about the general attitude our society has to sadness, I have noticed that while we seem to be quite good at finding reasons for sadness, we really have not spent much time simply describing or sharing our experiences of this natural human experience, let alone enquiring into how we can become more skilful at navigating it.

In our culture we define sadness too narrowly. We do not have enough words to describe the subtleties of sadness and the gifts it can bring. We do have the word 'melancholy'. It is a beautiful and poetic word but it's not in common use. Sometimes we use the phrase 'the blues', a musical and lyrical term that suggests many more soulful possibilities. However, in our day-to-day conversations we too quickly refer to our experience of sadness as 'depression', which automatically makes it part of ill-health and leads us to think of treatments involving medication. As adults, in our discomfort with sadness and grief (and also, of course, out of genuine concern), we want people to move out of the experience quickly, especially children and young people. Our growing awareness of youth depression and the unspeakable tragedy of youth suicide only increases our fear of *any* kind of sadness in young people, even if that sadness is actually the most appropriate response to a situation.

THE UNFATHOMABLE CHASM—MIRIAM

Sadness had no place in our family. In fact, feelings in general had no place. I rarely recall my brothers or sister or parents talking about what was happening inside. My father was an army man and he made it clear that feelings, whatever shade they came in, were completely irrelevant. Even though he was in great physical pain when I saw him for the last time a couple of years ago, he would be silent or leave the room if he felt any strong discomfort.

Two specific and extreme examples that illustrate how we all dealt with sadness are when my sister died and, then later, my mother. I was a teenager and the process of grieving was a very private affair. I recall closing my bedroom door and crying to myself when I heard my sister had died, and I know my mother did the same. There was never even any discussion about the circumstances of her death. Two years later when my mother died, I remember seeing my father looking down with an expression of sadness on his face. I think it was the first time I had ever seen him with such a reflective expression. But no one ever spoke about what they were feeling. The chasm was unfathomable.

A few weeks ago we had an assignment in the anthropology class I am taking. We had to discuss the theory that words create your reality, rather than the other way around. When I think about it, the word 'sadness' was not in our vocabulary. It was not discussed, and therefore it did not exist.

At what cost do we banish our sadness to the shadowy realms of non-existence?

Recently, I was chatting with a psychologist who works in a university about our lack of skill in dealing with sadness and our increasing tendency to reach for medication when confronted with any kind of internal discomfort. She said that over the years she had noticed a big rise in the number of student clients asking for antidepressants. Just prior to exam times, in particular, a steady stream of students sees her seeking medication. Previously her clients were more likely to want to discuss how they were feeling but now, she said, increasing numbers simply want a prescription. Of course, many of these students may genuinely need antidepressants, and thank goodness they feel able to seek help. But perhaps we do have to ask ourselves why we have become more comfortable in taking a medical approach when we feel stressed or emotional, rather than allowing these experiences a valued place at the table. These natural states do have a real purpose: they help teach us about resilience.

Clearly, there is a seriously debilitating illness called depression and it is a very good thing that as a society we are becoming more aware of the symptoms and effects of this illness. However, sadness and grief are not depression. While it is imperative that we respond to depression with more openness and skill, it is equally important that we bring greater depth to our understanding of the nuances of sadness, and the great opportunities that it can offer us, before automatically labelling it as depression.

When we turn sadness into a medical condition, and do not allow ourselves access to the deepening power of soulful melancholy, we can become angry, tired or very dry and brittle as a person. Depression or a serious addiction can be the result of *not* taking the time to acknowledge and learn from our experiences of sadness. By exploring the eddies and currents of sadness and becoming more skilled at learning how to recognise and harvest these times, I believe we can help head off or move out of depression.

There are many flavours and nuances of sadness. The word 'depression' does these states of being a great injustice. Even the word 'sadness' in the narrow sense that we currently understand it does not express the richness and promise contained within these experiences.

I must confess, though, that I like the word 'sadness'. It begins with a lovely 's' sound that reminds me of the many other words we can draw on to describe the shades of sadness—words that also contain the soft 's': soulful, wistful, subtle, seeking, sighing, solitary, silent, whispered, shaded, shadowed, salty, slow, still, soft, seed, supple, and even sweet. When we find the courage to admit it, the experience of soulful sadness can be very, very sweet . . . in a salty kind of way.

As we start to embrace the word sadness, we will see it grow with nuance. Then as we imbue it with richer and more compassionate layers of meaning and significance, its worth will become apparent to us. We will experience ourselves growing and expanding from within. We will increase our capacity to embrace our life, with all its ups and downs. We will become 'bigger' people.

Many of us, especially women, spend a lot of time and energy trying to grow smaller. Literally. We are always trying to lose weight and drop a dress size or two. Of course, there may be really good reasons for this. Not the least of which is how some of us look in Lycra. But I wonder what subtle effects this eternal quest for the shrinking woman has on us emotionally and even spiritually? Might it also be diminishing us, encouraging us to be smaller, to take up less room in other ways as well? What if we learned the art of growing *bigger* and gathering power from within—of letting our whole life, including our sadness, help us expand and fill up right to the edge of our skin?

Our attention has the power to help us do this. Our own big-hearted, courageous and respectful attention to everything we experience— the good, the bad, the ugly. . . and the just plain embarrassing—is very powerful. When we bring a steady, compassionate gaze to an experience instead of trying to simply make it go away, the emotion releases its stranglehold and it is as if a 'soul substance' is then released and made available to us. The result is that we grow bigger and fuller as people.

One way we can bring our big-hearted attention to sadness is to harness our own creativity. When creativity is added to the mix, sadness ceases to be a medical condition, but can become a larger-than-life character, a grand Diva who visits from time to time—dour and prickly she may be, but nevertheless regal and worthy of great respect. Perhaps we can think of her as the goddess 'Melancholia' who, like every self-respecting goddess, comes bearing gifts as well as challenges. She can be high maintenance but she is definitely worthy of the homage paid.

I wonder how your experience might subtly shift if you thought of your times of sadness as visits by Melancholia? What might she have to say to you when she comes calling? Perhaps she might say that it is time to reassess your goals, to have quiet 'down time', to heed her visit as a signal for change and growth. You might notice a pattern to her visits, such as a particular time of the year. She certainly possesses the power to take the wind out of your sails as she sweeps into the room calling for a time of stillness and retreat.

Clearly, there are times when we need to seek professional help for the serious illness of depression, or for the unfathomable and lingering sadness of grief and loss. But sometimes our wistful sadness, our soulful melancholy, is *not* depression or grief over a tragic loss. Our feelings of sadness may not necessarily signal something is going wrong. We may sense that a time of sadness is a call to reassess our goals and attitudes, a call for retreat—or perhaps it may signal a time of transition, a shift in our identity. Rather than experiencing our melancholy or sadness or the blues as a frightening illness, these times can be seen as full of potency and possibility. We may find ourselves wanting to take time to sit with our sadness, lean into it . . . let it become soulful.

> **A CONVERSATION WITH MELANCHOLIA**
>
> Are there times when you are especially prone to bouts of melancholy? A time of the day? A time of the month? A time of the year? A time of the season? When your tax is due?
>
> Can you see any pattern to your experiences of sadness?
>
> Think of these times as visits by the goddess Melancholia. What might she have to tell you about a time of sadness? What does she recommend you do?
>
> Imagine a conversation you might have with Melancholia. If you wish, you can write the dialogue down.

THE FIRST CUT—CLAIRE

Yesterday, I felt like I could hardly get motivated to set foot out of my bedroom. Heavy limbs. I felt menstrual as anything. I had that subtly enervating feeling of suspended animation accompanied by a high-pitched, continuous, yet inaudible note. Those hormones moaning. Felt like I could only bear the next moment if I was flat on my back and totally still. But I went through the motions of the day. Today the day is flowing just a tad more easily. Emphasis on 'just a tad'. My 18-year-old daughter had a final exam at noon today. Earlier in the day I drove her into town to meet her best friend for breakfast. As soon as we arrived she realised she had forgotten her phone—the phone she cannot be without. We drove home again and she went inside to get the wayward phone while I waited in the car. She came out wearing different clothes and off we went for Take Two; only to discover she still didn't have her phone. A U-turn and Take Three. Now she has the phone—the one she can't be without, especially now. You see, she broke up with her boyfriend two days ago and has a broken heart. I feel it too. I keep wanting to fix it up but, of course, it can't be done. Ahh, I feel sad.

Over a period of years, I began to watch my experience of sadness very closely. I noticed that whatever may have triggered an hour, day, week or longer period of sadness, each 'bout' seemed to cycle through seven phases. I wanted to describe this cycle so I honed in on how the feeling began, where it seemed to lead, how it subtly transformed and

> **RECALLING A MOMENT OF WISTFUL SADNESS**
> Gently recall a moment or two over the last few days when you felt a little sad or wistful. Just touch on this occasion very lightly. The feeling may have arisen while talking to someone, or while sitting quietly in a café, or thinking about someone you miss, or even looking at a beautiful sunset. Where were you? What was happening? How did you feel?
>
> Take a few seconds to remember the moment and describe it to yourself. Don't try to solve it or focus on the cause. Just let it arise and notice what the experience is like. Then sigh and let it fade. You may still feel the touch of soulful sadness even as the memory fades—a flower from the day.

what actions felt appropriate as it unfolded. I asked myself, 'How do I first know that soulful sadness is calling me?', 'What happens next?', 'How do I know when a particular cycle of sadness is complete?' And, finally, 'What's the point of it—what's it all for, anyway?'

My response to this last question is that as we explore soulful sadness, we begin to learn the dynamics of making happiness right here in our everyday lives; learning a little about how to transform the fruity mix of everyday life into something that can nourish us. It may seem contradictory at first, but learning to be with our sadness in skilful ways is a vital ingredient in learning how to be happy. It's a soulful way of living. We learn to become happier not by scrambling to make our sadness go away, but by taking some time to let our soulful sadness lead us through its natural cycle, and encouraging ourselves to flow with the phases of that cycle rather than getting stuck anywhere along the way.

As you become familiar with the cycle of soulful sadness you will see how you can apply it in your personal and professional life. You can use this cycle or adapt it to engage with feelings of disappointment or regret, or a whole range of other 'negative' experiences as well. As you explore the cycle, you will be tracking your own inner terrain and getting to know it a little better. You will be developing an important inner skill—the skill of harvesting your sadness.

What the cycle of soulful sadness doesn't offer are 'solutions' to sadness or formulas for keeping it lassoed, trussed up or hog-tied. On some level sadness has a habit of unseating us. Fortunately, we never quite get our sadness all neatly controlled even though we may wish we could. Each time we experience it, we revisit our own vulnerability. This is very humbling and, paradoxically, is actually its great strength. This humility brings us back into our hearts. It invites us to step back for a while from what we think we know and simply be still and open. We keep having to grow into our sad times to navigate them well. This is how soulful sadness helps us build soul. This approach to sadness rests on the transformative power of our big-hearted, creative and insightful attention to our experience of living. It is built on a profound trust that there is always a doorway of grace. It rests on the fundamental truth embodied in every authentic spiritual tradition: 'Seek and you will find.' There is a massive reservoir of wisdom within. Our role is to develop our capacity to turn to that and then apply what we discover in our lives.

CHAPTER 2

SOULFUL SADNESS

CHAPTER TWO

Like any emotion, it is difficult to capture in words exactly what sadness is, and yet most of us feel we know it in some form. You might be wondering what *soulful* sadness is. There is no single 'correct' definition. Each of us will bring our own nuances and experiences to our understanding of what it means and I am hoping that the term 'soulful sadness' will take on a deeply personal meaning for you.

Perhaps some comments about the word 'soul' might be a useful place to begin. To me this word means the essence of who *you* are as an individual—the unique and wondrous expression of you, like no other has ever been, or will ever be.

From this perspective, soul encompasses your personality, your stories, your dreams, your values, your sense of meaning and your life trajectory.

If soul is your unique identity and potential as an individual, then something becomes 'soulful' when it enables you to more fully uncover and express those things. Soulful activities build or uncover layers of richness and character.

They help round you out to the fullest expression of who you are given your unique emotional, physical and spiritual constitution, and the particular combination of experiences that come your way.

Here is a collection of comments that people have made about what the word soulful means to them:

'Something is soulful if it nurtures, enriches and waters as opposed to something that stunts, shrivels or causes brittleness.'
- 'Soulfulness is life-enhancing.'
- 'We experience something as soulful when we learn to distil it.'
- 'It is the quality of our attention that imparts soulfulness.'

- 'Soulfulness is gathered as we learn and grow from our experiences.'
- 'Soulfulness is when we give our permission for every aspect of our life to teach us.'
- 'Soulfulness is the accumulation of depth.'
- 'Soulfulness is gathered as we are made and unmade by everything in our life.'
- 'Soulfulness means reflecting quietly on what happens.'
- 'Soulfulness is a mood of the soul when it wants to know itself.'
- 'Soulfulness means you learn from everything, including difficult things.'
- 'Soulfulness isn't black and white; it comes with all the contradictions of being human so it contains vulnerability as well as strength.'
- 'Soulfulness is the deep enrichment that happens when life lives itself uniquely through us and we decide to be truly present for the ride.'

Drawing from these thoughts about the meaning of soulfulness we can say that sadness becomes soulful through our open-hearted engagement with it. It becomes soulful when we approach it consciously and respectfully in order to learn from it. Sadness releases its gifts when it is truly attended to.

To me, one of the main features of soulful sadness is a call for stillness and retreat. It is a time for pause and reflection. Poetry, music, drawing, writing and staring into space might be part of this time. Remembering and missing people and yearning for that indefinable something might also be present. Silence and solitude are often involved. Admitting that you are wrong and sighing may also be elements of the experience. Letting go is definitely a key feature. Feeling that, after all this time and after all that trying, you still don't know—wondering at the unsolvable mystery of it all—can be a prominent theme as well. Reassessing our goals and values and how we make meaning and choices for ourselves is also part of it. Anger and greed and envy are *not* part of it, but they can be features of the time before it; the second that these things are let go, the sweet state of soulful melancholy comes flooding in.

How is soulful sadness different from depression? There are always those blurry edges where one thing transitions to another, like the colours of the rainbow, like the family camping holiday that constant rain turns into a week-long nightmare, like the afternoon jaunt up a mountain that turns into the life-threatening climb from hell, like a bit of playful teasing that subtly moves into disrespect.

THE ART OF NAMING—KAZ

The day started rather well. Sailing through things on 'The List'. I went for my morning walk, got a coffee. Then it should have been the chores in town before going home to work. Suddenly, there it is, that tug of displacement, a wisp of free-floating discontent. My heart is suddenly and inexplicably heavy. Instantly, the wind goes out of my sails. Becalmed like the Ancient Mariner because of something he did wrong. My mind casts around for something to anchor the uncomfortable feeling to. I try to find a cause for it; something or someone to blame, starting with me. Maybe I made a mistake ending that relationship? What was I thinking doing that? Maybe I just don't know how to connect with people anymore? Probably never did, probably never will. Then on to someone else. Why aren't the cupboards painted like he promised so long ago? And by the way, why am I driving this dusty old paddock-basher of a car? Surely, that can't be right? Then I try on a few words to describe the feeling. Is it loneliness? Depression? Sadness? Abandonment? Or is it the opposite? Is this heaviness of heart actually fullness? Ripeness? Overflowing like the ache that comes with the let-down of breast milk. Is it love, bliss even?

I see in that moment that I can call it many things, and that what I choose to call it is the name it will answer to for a while. A whole drama will unfold from there. And I also see that beneath each of these names is a single essence: It's a call inside, a call of the soul to know itself. I decide not to name it anything but to simply allow it to be what it is—a pull inside. I abandon 'The List', drive home and sit quietly in my room, alone in the company of that call for a while. I am aware that it is such a privilege to be able to do this, and I am grateful. The rest of the day is tinged with self-containment and sacredness.

While clinical depression and our various experiences of sadness are not the same, there are those fuzzy transitions where one becomes the other. Though there may not always be crisp boundaries, I suspect we may instinctively know more about the differences between depression and soulful sadness than we think. If we explore our intuitive sense about the differences between soulful sadness and depression it will deepen our understanding of what soulful sadness means to us, and begin to build our skill in working with it. We will also be in a better position to recognise when we are stuck and need help.

Of course, everyone is different, and feelings can be particularly slippery. Two people might use very different words, images and expressions to describe their feelings. Even if they use the same words,

EXPLORING THE DIFFERENCES BETWEEN SOULFUL SADNESS AND DEPRESSION

We are going to make two mind maps: one for depression and one for soulful sadness. A mind map is a page filled with words all radiating out from a single word or phrase. It is a simple and fun way of gathering a lot of information about a topic very quickly.

Take two blank sheets of paper, or two facing pages of your journal, or use a whiteboard divided in half. In the middle of one sheet of paper write the word 'depression'. In the middle of the other write 'soulful sadness', or, if you prefer, 'soulful melancholy'.

Beginning with the page for depression, draw a short line anywhere out from the word and at the end of that line write another word that comes to mind. Circle that word, draw a line out from this second word and write a third word that comes to mind. Circle that word and connect it with a line to a fourth word. Keep going until your string of words comes to a natural end. Then return to the primary word, depression, and begin another string of connected and circled words. You will end up with several strings of connected words radiating out from depression.

Simply write down whatever comes to mind. Don't think about it too much. It can be useful to do it quite quickly. There are no right or wrong answers. You can be as clichéd or as inventive as you like. You may find you repeat words in the various strings; that's fine too. Feel free to let your creativity flow. The words you write might be colours, sounds, actions, images, metaphors, snippets of speech, even proverbs or sayings. They might be spelt incorrectly. They might be X-rated. They might be boring or intriguing or emotionally charged or strange. Some might not be words at all; they might be shapes, blotches, drawings.

When you feel that you have finished creating your depression mind map, do the same thing with 'soulful sadness'.

Now stand back and look at each of your mind maps in turn and consider the following:

- Are you surprised by any of the words you have written?
- Do any of the words seem particularly significant or intriguing? (If so, you may want to underline those words.)
- Are any words repeated? Can you see any particular themes?

Underline the word at the end of each string:

- Do the underlined words relate to each other?
- Have any of the thought strings taken you in unexpected directions?
- Is there one whole thought string in particular that feels definitive, significant or intriguing somehow?

Now compare the two mind maps:

- What are the differences and what are the similarities?
- Are there any words or images from each of the maps that could form a pair (either because they contrast as opposites, or because they seem to be close synonyms)?
- Did you notice any differences in how you felt constructing each of the maps?

Overall, how would you summarise the differences in flavour or feel between depression and soulful sadness?

they might interpret those words differently. What is adventurous for one person might be intimidating for another. What is rich and exciting for someone might be overwhelming for someone else. What seems pointless and boring for one person might be meaningful and soothing for another.

However, having pondered soulful sadness with many people, there do seem to be some points of agreement. One person told me that the words 'soulful sadness' and 'depression' gave rise to very different impressions in him. He said that depression felt frightening, as if possibilities were closing down, whereas soulful sadness felt like possibilities were opening up.

Another person described soulful sadness as moist and fertile while to her depression felt bitter, brittle and dry. Others have pointed to different colours—blacks, greys and dark blues for depression; and light blues, mauves, pale pinks or even white for soulful sadness.

Yet another person said that for her the word 'lonely' belonged with depression and the word 'aloneness' belonged with soulful melancholy. One man told me that, to him, blankness and shutting down were part of depression, while flashes of memory from his childhood accompanied by a wistful feeling were part of soulful melancholy.

THE WAKE-UP CALL—WILL

To me depression is dark, dense and static. I feel gutted. I feel bogged down and exhausted. It's like trying to walk through quicksand. When it gets really bad, I stop being able to feel anything at all apart from a freewheeling sense of hopelessness.

To me soulful sadness is dark too, but softer and accompanied by a feeling of slowly getting traction for decisions and changes I'm getting ready to make.

I'd never want to say that I know how to stop the feeling of sadness turning into depression. What a joke! But I am starting to get a bit of a handle on it. It's got something to do with getting very real and respectful when sadness comes. Like a wake-up call. That's what I'm starting to do now. To be honest, after last year, I'm too scared not to.

Sometimes images can communicate so much more about our feelings than words, and placing two images side by side can be a useful way of illustrating the differences between soulful sadness and depression. Cartoonists sometimes capture the fertile territory of soulful sadness beautifully. This is one of the reasons their work touches our hearts so deeply with just a few simple lines on paper. There is a cartoon by Michael Leunig that does this for me; it shows a man kneeling in front of a pot plant with his head bowed. Tears are falling one by one from his closed eyes into soil around the plant. The stem of the plant has a heart blooming at the top. A small sickle of a moon is in the background. The man's tears are watering a growing heart.

Another very different image by Matthew Johnstone captures the experience of depression equally well. This cartoon shows a man dressed in blue with a slightly shocked expression and downturned mouth encased in the middle of a huge block of ice. Circling the block of ice and looking at the suspended man is a black dog, a common image for depression. The block of ice has some hairline cracks in it, hinting at the faint possibility of the ice cracking. But for now, the man is completely frozen, cut off and incapacitated by the icy depression he is experiencing.

Both of these cartoons depict pain but the crucial difference is that in the Leunig image the tears of the crying man are nurturing a growing heart. An everyday miracle is occurring: sadness is being transmuted into growth. To me, this process of transmutation is the essence of soulfulness. I believe that we can become more skilful at bringing this quality of growth to our experiences of sadness. We begin by simply becoming more familiar with the nature of soulful sadness.

Times of soulful sadness can be entered into with softness and sacredness. They need not be dramatised or turned into a soap opera. They can be honoured as moments when deep listening and change can occur. There is a knack in reaping the fruits of these times, though. We can learn how to offer ourselves to our experience of soulful sadness more fully. We can invite ourselves to let go and ease back into our own skin. Most often, when experiencing sadness, we become afraid or impatient and we try to grasp onto the next moment or the next activity. Often, we try to lose ourselves in busy-ness—anything for a bit of distraction. You may notice this at play in your own life—I certainly do in mine! We notice a tiny twinge of something uncomfortable inside and our knee-jerk reaction might be to jump up and phone someone, or open the fridge door and graze, or watch TV, or rush from activity to activity rather than simply being still. Many people are desperately afraid of being alone for even an hour or two, and arrange their lives so that this rarely happens. It is as if we are trying to silence the noise of our own wheels with the clamour of external activity. But if we cannot be still and face our own company with gentleness and openness, how are we going to learn to experience lasting peace and joy within our own being?

> **CREATING YOUR IMAGE OF SOULFUL SADNESS**
>
> Create an image that expresses soulful sadness to you. You may want to cut out pictures from magazines and create a collage. You can paint or draw with pencils, pens, charcoals, watercolours or oils. You can create washes of colour or use pieces of coloured paper or fabric, stickers, sequins, ribbon and yarn glued to the page. You can include photographs (perhaps of a scene from nature or of someone—you?—in a reflective pose), or words, colours, shapes or themes you identified in your mind map.
>
> Please don't think you have to be 'an artist' to do this. No one else has to see this image unless you want to show it to them. It doesn't have to be 'good' or clever. Simply assemble a few bits and pieces for your collage or image (if you wish, you can do this very cheaply from the stationery section of bargain-basement stores) and let yourself play and have some fun. It might be very simple—a few images from a magazine or greeting card stuck to a page with sticky tape, and maybe a word or two scribbled somewhere on the page—or much more elaborate. When you have finished, place this image on your shelf, noticeboard or desk. By focusing on the nature of soulful sadness, by reflecting on its flavours, we are invoking these qualities and building our capacity to bring them to our experiences of sadness.

As well as responding to sadness with frantic busy-ness, many of us try to work it out with our intellect, as if sadness is a problem that we have to solve. But sometimes our analytical mind isn't all that helpful—we can't always work things out that way. We end up going round and round with the same old thoughts and strategies that don't really serve us that well anymore. Perhaps sometimes our experience of sadness just has to be accepted and experienced. It is like a companion or a visitor that we must walk alongside for a time.

When sadness arises it is very easy to think that it should not be happening and that something has gone wrong for us in a very personal way. However, it is important to realise that it is not always personal sadness that we are feeling, and neither is it wrong. Sometimes we are tuning into events that affect communities locally, nationally or globally. Sadness is an appropriate emotion to experience in the face of wider issues, such as the loss of species and the increase in pollution, violence, poverty, disease, war, crime and cruelty, in many forms.

For a long time I woke up every morning feeling such sadness and yet nothing was wrong in my life. I had not lost a child or experienced violence or disease or tragic loss. I was happy with my home and my relationships and yet I felt wounded and grieving. One day I had a dream in which a wise woman said, 'You should visit sick children in hospital.' I pondered this for a long time. I could not see how it was possible. I had two small children and no car and I lived in a street that was not close to public transport. I didn't think I should take the instruction literally, but I intuitively felt it pointed to an important direction in my life and so was a highly significant message to decipher.

Without ever understanding the instruction in that dream intellectually, I believe it has borne fruit. That time of morning sadness prompted me to begin a long contemplation of the uses of sadness. This contemplation has led me to believe that it is valuable to be able to feel our own sadness as well as empathise with the sadness of others; not to be drowned in sorrow, not to be overwhelmed by those feelings and unclear of where our personal boundaries and responsibilities lie, but as a way of understanding that we are intimately connected to everyone else and to the natural world. Being present and awake to what is happening in other people's lives and allowing their feelings to take on some reality for us is part of coming into the fullness of soul.

Above all soulful melancholy asks you to sit back deeply into yourself. Soulful sadness is a call to quiet reflection, a letting go of action and busy-ness, a time to turn inside and be present with yourself. These times of stillness with soulful sadness help to create room for hopeful possibilities to emerge in the fullness of time. Your moments of quiet attention to soulful sadness may be long or short. You may want to put aside an evening or two, a whole quiet weekend, or perhaps some daily quiet time in your room or garden. You may want to paint and draw and listen to beautiful music. Or simply sit or lie in stillness. You may want to take a meandering walk, look at the night sky, feed the ducks at the park or sit alone in a café. You may want to practise returning to stillness in short snippets throughout the day, such as while you are on the bus, in a queue, walking to the train station, feeding your baby. It is not so much what you do, but your inward focus and quiet attention that will soften the edges of your sadness and carry you through its soulful cycle. At the times of your choosing, simply allow your attention to be drawn inside. Notice how your soulful sadness is sitting within. Notice your breathing, your heart subtly pulsing, the sound in your ears. Sometimes it is helpful to say to the sadness, 'Ah, hello Quiet Companion. Here I am.' Simply be there.

For most of us, however, it is not always an easy thing to simply 'be there'. A special kind of effort is required to seek out quiet times and let go of busy-ness. Even when you are in your quiet place or engaged in your peaceful activity, you may notice the impulse to leap up and do the next thing. Simply sigh as the impulse comes swooping through and let it swoop on out, without you. You don't need to take the bait, you can take a raincheck, you can pass up the impulse to leap to the next thing. You can offer it up—and it truly is an offering, a sacred sacrifice even. In soulful sadness you are sitting still, releasing the urge to race off here, go there, act on this, change that. You must have noticed that when you are caught up doing these things the 'good thing' you are trying to grasp evaporates under the heat generated by the doing. In letting go and being present with your soulful sadness you are saying, 'Right here, right now, right in these circumstances, is what I need.' With the sweet effort of this letting go your soulful sadness will begin to sing for you.

What will that song be about, I wonder? What are the uses of soulful sadness? Is it just some random thing from the rag-and-bone shop of life? Do we just put up with it for a while and sigh with relief when it's gone—until next time?

We can receive so much more from our experiences of sadness than that. After sitting attentively with sadness while it takes us through its subtle phases, renewal becomes possible. We seem to access a deeper part of ourselves that enables us to become just that little bit bigger, that little bit more compassionate. A time of soulful sadness enriches us from within—and then, when the world calls us to outer action once again, we bring what we have gained with us.

CHAPTER 3

THE CYCLE OF SOULFUL SADNESS

CHAPTER THREE

Our world is filled with cycles: the cycle of the seasons, of the tides, of the incoming and outgoing breath, of sleep. There are beginnings, middles and endings in relationships, projects and almost everything we do. So, too, with soulful sadness.

In the late 1960s and '70s some groundbreaking work was done in the area of bereavement by Elisabeth Kübler-Ross. This work made an enormous contribution to our understanding of grieving as a journey that shifts and changes. While every individual is different and their experience does not always follow a rigid formula, countless people have been assisted by understanding more about the stages of grief. It has given them solace to be able to recognise themes in their experience. For many people who are grieving, this can make all the difference in being able to put one foot in front of the other.

Soulful sadness, too, seems to move through a discernible cycle. While everyone's experience is unique, there are ways in which our encounters with soulful sadness tend to follow a pattern with distinct changes in flavour along the way. Noticing this cycle, naming the phases within it, and beginning to understand the invitations that are present within each of these stages has been extremely helpful to me in learning to engage with my own experiences of sadness without panicking or feeling stranded and freezing into depression. The cycle of soulful sadness presented later in this chapter is intended as a map for awareness rather than a set of hard and fast rules or formulas. I hope you will find it useful for getting to know your own landscape of soulful sadness.

Especially in times of sadness and difficulty it can be deeply reassuring to observe the naturally-occurring cycles around us. They remind us that everything is in a process of change and that, given time, even the most acute emotion will subtly shift. They remind us that decay and dissolution have their place in the process just as much as new growth and fresh bursts of hope.

> **NOTICING NATURAL CYCLES**
>
> Find objects that represent cycles to you—perhaps a shell with a spiral shape, or something that is round like a stone, a metal spring or twisted wood. It might be a series of connected objects such as a seed, a leaf and a flower; or a design on a piece of fabric or paper; maybe a painting or image on a postcard; it could be a piece of weathered bone or glass.
>
> You could also create an object that represents cycles to you, such as a chain of coloured paper clips, daisy flowers or paper circles. Or it could be a ring or ball of wire, a pipe cleaner in the shape of an infinity sign, a wreath of ivy or willow. You may want to draw or paint symbols such as spirals, circles, Celtic knots or phases of the moon. You may want to fill a small box with sand and use your fingers or a stick to create circular patterns.
>
> Clear a small space on a shelf, on a desk, on a window ledge, on a mantel, or even outside in the garden. Place these objects there. Arrange them in a way that is pleasing to you.
>
> By bringing an appreciative eye to the cycles around you in this way, you are honing your capacity to notice the subtle shifts in your own internal cycles and preparing yourself to flow through them with a more expanded and easeful attitude.

BURYING BONES—LUKE

Dogs seem to know intuitively about cycles; it's wired into their DNA. They bury bones to come back to in leaner times. This has been a very effective survival strategy for them over centuries. Not sure that it's terribly conscious, though. Our dog buries pieces of toast. Trots up the dirt road, toast between the jaws and buries it in the top paddock. She keeps on doing it even though it is a singularly ineffective strategy. The decomposition cycle happens too fast. Nothing to harvest when she comes back to the burial site.

The kids did it when they were little, too. They mixed up weird concoctions of flour, juice, petals and cocoa which they called 'Maan'. Then they poured it into hollowed-out watermelon halves, froze them in the freezer, then buried them. Three weeks later they dug up the slushy mess to see how it had transformed. All in the interests of science.

Moral of the story: some things, like sadness, are best not buried too deep and abandoned for too long; they may not harvest well later. However, like wine, a bit of careful preparation and tending in a dark place can be very fruitful.

In our daily life, just when we think we have something nailed, it shifts and changes—like that elusive quality, 'balance'. We seem to hit the sweet spot of equilibrium, then almost immediately we need to adjust one way or the other, like a yacht tacking from side to side so it can go forward.

Life is in constant flux and learning to skilfully navigate those subtle (or massive) shifts is a lifelong learning process. So too with sadness. When we look carefully at soulful sadness we see that the mood of it shifts and we begin to recognise the signposts along the way. We learn a little more about what is useful for us to do in each of the phases of soulful sadness; what actions serve us and are in tune with our own inner experience.

In English the word 'sadness' is a noun; it communicates that sadness is a thing. However, other languages can help us think about it differently. According to early twentieth-century linguist Benjamin Lee Whorf, in the Hopi language, many things that English speakers regard as objects are thought of by the Hopis as actions. For example, in English the word 'fist' means a balled-up hand but in Hopi it is considered an action, something you do—and the word for it is more like 'fisting'.

How would it be if we thought of 'sadness' as 'sadding'? This might help us to relate to this natural human experience as a cycle or journey, and we might be more inclined to notice the patterns and signposts along the way.

The seven-stage cycle below is a map of the terrain of soulful melancholy as I experience it. Another person might easily look inside themselves and see the cycle differently. They might divide up the phases in quite another way, perhaps coming up with fewer or larger numbers of phases, perhaps identifying different flavours and themes. It doesn't really matter.

By consciously engaging with each phase of the cycle, you will find that your understanding and experience of sadness are greatly enriched, and you are better able to harness the gifts of this natural human experience and make skilful choices in your life. And you can share your increased capacity and understanding with others, perhaps especially with the young people around you. Even if you don't consciously choose to do this, you will be doing it simply because of the way they see you carry yourself through your own sad places at home and in the workplace. This is very important—it can make all the difference, not just in your own life, but in someone else's as well.

Using this cycle of soulful sadness you will be getting to know your sadness more intimately, and therefore you will be far less prone to getting lost in the experience. You will be better able to access the power of your own compassionate and refined attention. You will be practising the gentle art of transforming your experiences of sadness. Who knows what you might discover along the way about the uses of sadness? Perhaps you will learn to be less afraid of sadness and more gracious when sadness comes calling.

CYCLE OF SOULFUL SADNESS

1. The Soul Calls
2. Entering Liminal Space
3. Attending to Stillness
4. Encountering Grace
5. Embracing Contradictions
6. Befriending Yourself
7. The World Calls

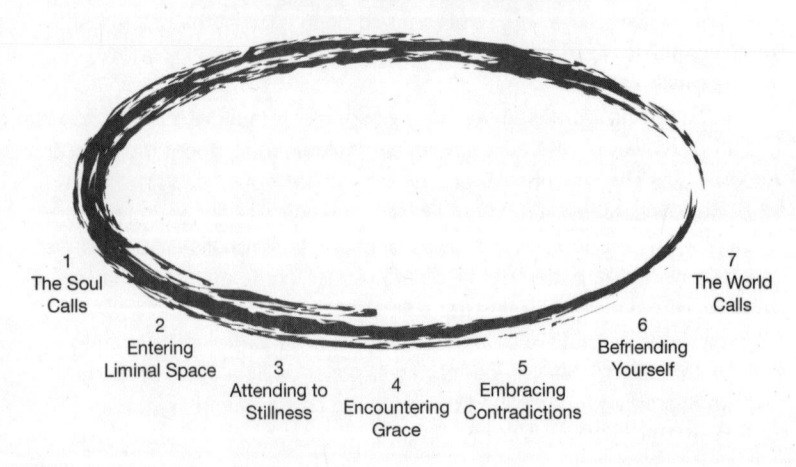

You can see that the cycle begins with 'The Soul Calls' and ends with 'The World Calls'. This is because, to me, soulful sadness arises out of the interplay between these two divine calls. The call of the soul pulls us inside for a time of reflection and pause, then as we give our attention and permission to that process we move through the cycle and are naturally drawn towards active engagement with the world once again.

Some time later, something may not go according to plan, the world somehow disappoints us or we grow jaded once more. This suggests there is something more for us to learn. Again we become aware of the call of our soul and another cycle of soulful sadness begins, culminating in the last phase where we are drawn back to apply our learning in our world.

This cycle describes a very profound way in which we can learn and grow and share with others. It invites us to truly imbibe our insights about sadness and bring them forward into our lives so that we and others can be enriched by them. Our journey through the cycle comprises seven phases of soulful sadness.

1 THE SOUL CALLS—LONGING

Somehow, nothing has quite turned out the way I expected. I have tried really hard, given it my best shot, but somehow, even the good things seem tinged with disappointment. It's time to let go of rushing around and to be still. Something's calling me from within. I am yearning for something. I am longing for something. I am homesick. Even though I am at home, still I am yearning for my true home. I see and hear that longing everywhere: I think of soulful calls—like the call of a whale, the mournful sound of a single tuba, and a ship's foghorn in the mist. Images like an eagle circling on the thermals. It's time to pause and be alone.

The soul is calling me.

2 ENTERING LIMINAL SPACE—NOT KNOWING

I have to admit, I have no answers. I truly don't know what move to make next, what decision to make. I sigh. I let go. I just don't know. I am in between. Suspended. I don't know the way forward, the way back, or even how I got here. I might even say, 'I give up', 'What's the point?' and 'Is change really possible?' I don't know if it will all work out or not. I can't pretend. The old answers no longer seem to hold water. There aren't any new ones to put in their place either. I have to sit in this not knowing, and wait. I gently simmer. Endurance. Courage. The long note.

The truth is, I just don't know.

3 ATTENDING TO STILLNESS—DEEP LISTENING

As I accept not knowing and simply wait, I begin to listen beyond my own thoughts and feelings. I notice the throb of my blood in my ears. I hear my breath coming in and going out. I fall into the sounds of silence. The creaking of the house, the sound of traffic in the distance. I fall into quiet daydreams in random places. I linger in the car after parking it. I read poetry, write in my journal, listen to music, stare at the fire, say a prayer. I am slow to return phone calls. I am in retreat. The more I listen, the stiller I become, and somehow the longing begins to sweeten. My own pat answers have fallen away and I want to attend more carefully to each moment. I am a little more humble and I begin to open to the possibility that I can learn. I begin to really listen to people when they talk, notice signs, attend to stillness.

I become still enough to truly listen.

4 ENCOUNTERING GRACE—THE TURNING POINT

As I arrive more fully in the present moment, I notice that it's okay. More than okay; it's actually benevolent. Suddenly, I encounter a 'happening', a moment of beauty, a sight that moves me, a thought that uplifts me and fills my heart. A red balloon floating away in the blue sky, a genuine smile on someone's face, a dog wagging its entire back end in welcome, something a person says, a flash of insight, the sight of someone really trying, a numberplate with an unexpected message, the way the curtain wafts. Perhaps for the tiniest moment, I encounter something sacred. For a time, even a second or two, my mind stops in its tracks and is amazed. Gravity releases me. I let go. I am effortlessly supported. What a relief. I drink in this life-giving nourishment. In the afterglow of that encounter what I say and do is perfectly in tune. My whole being is watered, softened and expanded.

I am moved and nothing is quite the same.

5 EMBRACING CONTRADICTIONS—HOLDING THE OPPOSITES

Touched by that encounter, my mind can bring me treasures now. I see with compassionate eyes. I see that most of the time we are all trying our best. Things are far more layered than I thought. For now, I am able to let go of control and perfection, and I am released from my own harsh judgement. I have stopped thinking in terms of black or white, right or wrong, good or bad. I see that beauty and sadness are forever mixed. Love and hate, happiness and sadness, pleasure and pain, and all the opposites are always at play. Each is an aspect of the other. I can feel them all at the same time. I am both happy and sad . . . and all is well. This is the way it is.

I am big enough to hold the opposites.

6 BEFRIENDING YOURSELF—MAKING CONSCIOUS CHOICES

Even though I can see that everything has a place at the table and there are endless possibilities, I cannot choose them all. Some things will serve and some will not. I must apply a discerning eye. I stand back now and take stock of what is important to me. Each of my actions has consequences and I want to choose wisely and gather my will. I identify my cherished values. I review my actions and habits. I assess which actions are truly authentic for me, and which ones aren't. Which ones reflect my values and make my heart sing? I know ultimately it is up to me to make my life meaningful. I view all this with soft and loving eyes, knowing that I will sometimes stumble. I speak kindly to myself and am my own best friend.

I am responsible for the choices and meaning in my life.

7 THE WORLD CALLS—OFFERING

With greater clarity I walk forward and engage with my world. I greet the moment with a renewed sense of hope and optimism. Many possibilities and ideas are emerging and I make plans to implement them skilfully. I relish questions and spark creatively with others. My actions are conscious and bright. I have something to offer and I look forward to making a contribution. I consider my life's purpose and sharpen my intention. I welcome my own leadership and the leadership of others. I feel courageous, energetic and centred. I am ready to participate, engage and offer my service generously.

The world is calling me.

A WHISTLE STOP AT EACH STATION

Find a room where you can sit quietly on your own without being interrupted for for half an hour, perhaps with a cup of tea or glass of something fresh. When you have settled in, read aloud the summary of each of the seven phases above, pausing silently for a while after each one to feel it out and sense its quality. Take your time. Notice any thoughts, feelings, images and words that arise as you sit quietly after reading each phase out loud.

When you have completed all seven, sit quietly for a moment or two and see if you can begin

> to get a sense of the flow and movement of the cycle as a whole. It doesn't matter if anything is unfamiliar or unclear. This is your first sweep through. Don't try to force yourself to 'get it' or hold it in your mind all at once. Just notice what you notice. Then, if you like, you can pick up your pen and make a few notes in your journal.

As human beings our internal processes are rarely all neat and tidy like a diagram. We need powerful images and symbols to capture the depth of our feeling and the complexity of feeling several emotions at once. So rather than being a rigid blueprint, the cycle of soulful sadness is a loose pattern for how a time of soulful sadness tends to play out. The seven phases are fluid signposts and our experiences of them will vary. For example, it may take a couple of weeks, months, or even longer to move through all the phases. Or it can happen over a day, an afternoon, an hour or even within the flash of a few minutes.

One person told me that she is able to visualise the flow of the whole cycle by imagining a mime artist on a stage. She 'sees' him with white paint on his face, silently expressing each phase in the cycle through postures and gestures.

As he begins to feel the sadness and the longing of his soul, his shoulders sag and his head bows and his hand goes to his heart; as he enters the liminal space of not knowing he raises his head and looks out at the audience expressing his bewilderment with raised eyebrows and open palms; then he lowers his hands and becomes perfectly still as he begins to listen intently, gazing into the distance with his head cocked slightly to one side; then something captures his attention and his back lengthens, his chest expands and his face opens in delight as he encounters a moment of insight; then his posture expands even more and he stretches out his arms as he takes in the huge array of opposites; then he settles back down into himself, considering each possibility in turn and getting ready to make his conscious choices; finally, he rises to his full height, engages with the audience through kind eyes, and stands for a moment feeling the power of his own presence within his open posture, before moving in a particular direction in a purposeful manner.

ONE SIMPLE THING—MARCUS

The other day at work I led a team-building activity that didn't go as well as I had hoped. People began giving me feedback about what didn't work for them and, even though it was gentle and respectful, I felt a flash of annoyance. I felt my posture subtly stiffen as I was about to leap in and defend myself. Then, almost instantly, I reminded myself to listen to what they were saying. I sat back and breathed out. My shoulders deflated ever so subtly. And immediately, there it was arising from within me: the bitter–sweet feeling of soulful sadness replacing the initial agitation.

I thought, 'Here we are again, life is just so unfathomable. The truth is, what I tried really didn't work that well. It's such a mystery how to facilitate change. I thought I could fix this team up! But I actually don't have any cute, pat answers. Let me really listen to others and try to learn.'

From there I began to think about one simple thing that I could do each day that encapsulates what is important to me in how I am in this team.

In the example above, you can see how Marcus rapidly cycles through the phases of soulful melancholy (not necessarily in any strict order)—the sting of things not going according to plan, admitting that you don't know and choosing to listen, encountering insight, thinking about what is important, and so on. You can see how he finds humility and the desire to change himself rather than trying to change others. He told me this whole internal process took about fifteen minutes during the meeting. (You never know what is going on for someone below the surface in a meeting!) It took a day or so after that to finally settle on what he wanted to do at work that would reflect his values and goodwill. And that was simply to greet each person in the team every morning before he turned on his computer. In this way he used a difficult experience to come to a beautifully simple meaning-making action.

While a cycle of soulful sadness can happen very quickly and be relatively easy, it can also take quite a while and draw on every ounce of your courage and heart. You may not spend equal amounts of time in each of the phases. Some of the phases may be very short, as if you are hardly touching on them at all, and some may be quite long. You may find that you are in the liminal phase—simply not knowing—for quite a long time. Just hanging in and hanging in with it. At some point, you may even want to deliberately encourage yourself to move on to the next phase, and being familiar with the cycle will give you some clues about what activities will help you do that.

The phases themselves may not always be clear-cut and separate. You may feel that you just don't know (Entering Liminal Space) and that you are deeply listening (Attending to Stillness) at the same time; you may feel that you are focusing on reviewing what is of great value to you (Befriending Yourself) and being pulled towards your service in the world (The World Calls) simultaneously.

As you will discover, the cycle doesn't necessarily play out in strict order. You may feel you are done with a particular phase only to find yourself right 'back' there again. You may become very clear about what actions you need to take, then suddenly you can't think for the life of you why you would even dream of being sure about anything. You may even think, 'Oh – My – God! Here I am again right back in not knowing a single thing.' Once more, you are called upon to sit in that space until there is a subtle shift and you become drawn into deep listening again.

While all these variations may happen, the phases are valuable signposts to help us navigate the landscape of sadness and tolerate (perhaps even savour) the dirt roads, back lanes, wheel spins and misty weather along the way. When entered into with respect and gentleness, a cycle of soulful melancholy enriches us and eventually leads us back to engagement with life and community. It helps us to uncover hopeful possibilities and engage in actions that more fully reflect our deeply held values. The following seven chapters explore each of the phases in the cycle in detail.

CHAPTER 4

THE SOUL CALLS—LONGING

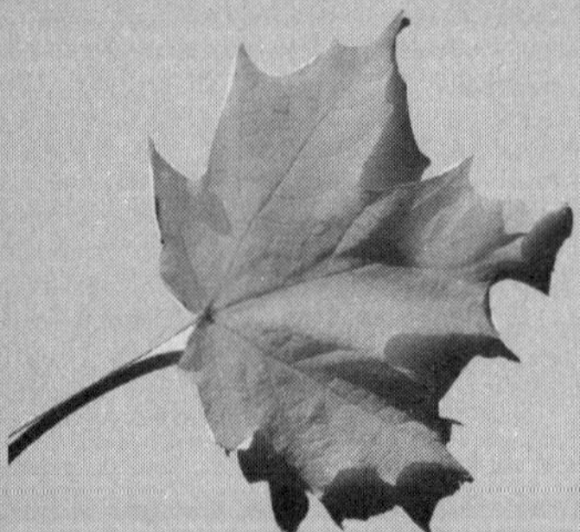

CHAPTER FOUR

The first flush of soulful sadness is sometimes ushered in by disappointment. As anyone living on the planet for more than five minutes knows, things don't always go according to plan. Despite all our effort, skills and resources, sometimes things just don't work out the way we hoped. Even when events *do* unfold exactly as we planned, our anticipated feeling of fulfilment may simply be a sorry whimper after a very little bang. This can happen when a long-planned holiday doesn't quite deliver the relaxation, renewal and sheer pleasure we anticipated it would. Or when we do not get the job we applied for, or when our attempts to mend a relationship are unsuccessful.

Even with our best endeavours we may make a fool of ourselves, do something hurtful that we later regret, or find ourselves backsliding from that New Year's resolution (the same one we made last year). We may have blown a chance to parent well, made a decision we are not proud of, witnessed an unkindness, or felt let down, betrayed or passed over. Or in a moment of clarity we suddenly glimpse our own part in pollution, war and homelessness.

Why would these experiences *not* be a matter of sadness? In all these and countless other ways we cannot seem to be the person or the society we truly want to be—we face our own disappointment. But the most interesting question here is, what really creative and truly uplifting thing will we do with our disappointment and sadness? We can make it soulful by giving it our attention and letting it lead us naturally to the best action we can muster.

Disappointment, regret or frustration can initiate a period

of soulful sadness. However, the first stage of soulful sadness can also arise, not because something has gone awry, but because life is moving on and you are called upon to make a shift: when your son or daughter is leaving home, at menopause, when a baby is born, when you move house, when you retire, when a disease takes up residence in your body, when you emigrate, when a relationship ends. Along with these times of change you may experience a call for greater authenticity or an invitation to adjust your attitudes, actions and beliefs. Often our first inkling of such a call is a feeling of sadness.

Sometimes a cycle of soulful melancholy is preceded by exhaustion. It is as if, eventually, in some very mysterious way, *all* 'doing' grows jaded and tainted. Even the most magnificent banquet loses its appeal when you have eaten your fill. After all your shiny resolutions have dulled a little, after plans and strategies have been acted upon with as much skill as you can muster, after many insights have arisen, after all the huffing and puffing, after the pleasure of gaining ground and achieving some goals, and the inevitable loss of ground with others . . . we wind down and stop. We may even feel that all our actions, both good and bad, have turned to clay. Ashes to ashes, dust to dust.

We may be surprised, resigned, faintly bewildered, foot-stampingly annoyed, disappointed, pleased or simply tired. We know that something is up; something is chaffing, something is calling us to become still. What is it that wants our attention?

It is the call of our own soul.

Over quite a few years now I have asked myself and many others, 'What is the first thing you notice; how do you know that you are entering a cycle of soulful melancholy?' People speak of longing, yearning and of homesickness. Even though we speak about it in many different ways, everyone seems to recognise it. This longing. This yearning.

Here are some of the ways people have described it:

- 'feeling that something is missing';
- 'a deep pull for wholeness';
- 'the desire to merge';
- 'longing for peace';
- 'wanting to feel truly satisfied';
- 'wanting to be alone';
- 'feeling like I want to pray even though I don't believe in God';
- 'feeling ready to face something';

- 'wanting to get off the merry-go-round for while';
- 'not wanting to figure it all out anymore, just wanting to be quiet';
- 'wanting to listen to sad music and write poetry';
- 'wanting to rest in my heart';
- 'feeling like I need to get really honest with myself';
- 'wishing I could truly let go';
- 'wanting to feel I truly belong';
- 'sighing all the time and wanting to withdraw';
- 'longing for fulfilment';
- 'wanting to just stop';
- 'wanting to feel complete';
- 'wishing I knew how to be myself'; and
- 'longing for that indefinable thing'.

Longing seems to be part of being human. Spiritual traditions have long revered longing as that which draws us into our own being and into a spiritual life. Sometimes a sound like a foghorn in the mist or a sight such as snow melting awakens this feeling of longing in us. Sometimes it arises in the most ordinary of situations, most often in a moment of solitude—even in the midst of a crowd. Children naturally know this experience of longing, even though they may not be able to put it into words.

THE CLIMBING FRAME—BENNY

I was ten years old and sitting quietly in a classroom while the teacher was reading aloud to the class. Out in the playground beyond the classroom window was a metal climbing frame. A slight breeze was causing a small length of chain to clang gently against the metal frame. Clang . . . clang . . . clang. As I listened to this random yet repeated sound, the classroom scene receded and I drifted into space. I felt peaceful but something else was also in that feeling that I couldn't describe.

Looking back I think it was longing. I wasn't longing *for* anything in particular; it was pure longing on its own.

May no one throw a piece of chalk at a child rendered silent by the gentle power of a random, faraway sound. Daydreaming and staring into space may sometimes be the most important learning that is going on in a classroom!

> **A MEMORY OF SWEET LONGING**
> Think back to your time as a child. Can you remember a moment when you experienced a sweet and perhaps even slightly aching longing? *Not* a moment of hurt, but a moment when you felt your heart or soul gently calling you. Perhaps it was while sitting in a classroom daydreaming, lying on the grass looking up at the shape of the clouds, staring up at the night sky, high up in a tree or deep in a secret hiding place. Where were you? Were you alone? What was that feeling like? What was special about it?
>
> Take some time to describe it in your journal. You may want to simply note down a few key words or sentences, or you may want to describe it through a poem or a short story. As you recall and write about your experience, can you get closer to putting your finger on what the experience of longing feels like? What words would you use to describe it? What factors do you think contributed to this experience arising?

It can be quite difficult to describe that sweet and yet somehow painful feeling of longing in words. Once again languages other than our own offer us opportunities to step outside our usual ways of describing sadness and longing. They help us to capture some of the subtle flavours of this fundamental human experience.

There is a Celtic word, *hiraedd* (pronounced hir-aye-ith), that is often translated as 'homesickness', but it also means much more than that. It contains the sense of missing something that we may never have known—or missing something that is so deeply part of our past that we struggle to remember it clearly. Like the yearning we experience from time to time that feels ancient, as if we were remembering and longing for a wholeness we experienced long, long ago. Someone once likened it to the almost (but not quite) recoverable memory of our mother's heartbeat while we were in the womb.

The French have the phrase *nostalgie de la boue*, which literally means 'aching for the mud'. It can also be translated as 'wishing you could be off having a heedless romp in the country'. This puts a fun spin on the experience of longing—and those who are heading off to a boring meeting at work may well wish for it!

French also gives us *dépaysé*, which means 'de-countried' or not being in one's own country. This 'longing for country' is a very sad feeling filled with love and loss and grief that many indigenous people describe in relation to the dispossession of their traditional lands. Longing can truly contain this depth of grief.

In German there is the word *fernweh*, 'longing to be away'—the yearning to be somewhere other than here. This word can be thought of as the true opposite of *heimweh*, a German word meaning 'homesick' or longing for one's home. Both these words, even though they are opposites, contain flavours of longing.

Like Benny's story of listening to the metal chain clanging against the climbing frame, longing is sometimes triggered by something we hear. It can also arise from something we see, taste, smell or touch. It can range from something extraordinary and out of this world, such as the image of planet Earth from space, to everyday experiences like the hoot of an owl, or a snippet of music drifting out of a window.

> **THINGS THAT AWAKEN LONGING IN YOU**
>
> List things that awaken bitter-sweet longing within you. Begin with sounds. Is there a particular piece of music? A particular bird call or instrument? Think about places (or buildings or rooms), sights (perhaps from nature, like rain running down a window), images (such as a photograph), objects (such as a lock of hair or an abandoned suitcase), tastes, smells, situations, or even sayings such as Ned Kelly's 'Such is life'. Once you start listing things, you may find that memories of sights, sounds and smells from your childhood surface, bringing that feeling of sweet longing with them. Let your imagination play. Enjoy the range, poignancy and perhaps beauty of the images you conjure up.

Here are some things people have said awaken soulful longing in them:
- 'the coastline slowly darkening to a silhouette at nightfall';
- 'an eagle circling on the thermals';
- 'the faraway sound of a lawnmower in summer';
- 'whales calling';
- 'bagpipes';
- 'an athlete crawling over the line in a marathon';
- 'overgrown graves in a heritage graveyard';
- 'tibetan prayer flags fluttering on a rocky outcrop';
- 'the scent of lavender like my grandma used to wear';
- 'a ship slipping out of port';
- 'icebergs drifting';
- 'a leaf spiralling silently to the forest floor';
- 'Incense smoke curling gracefully in the air';
- 'an old gardening shoe that has permanently taken the shape of someone's foot';
- 'a room where a party has taken place and all the guests have left';
- 'sunset';
- 'the lull after making love';
- 'the sound of a violin being played in the distance';
- 'a sleeping baby'; and
- 'an empty swing moving slightly in the breeze'

These images show how linked beauty and soulful sadness can be. A list like this can be read like a poem, awakening a highly visual experience of stark beauty along with a feeling of sadness and longing.

While the experience of longing can be described as soft, it does have a fire to it, an edge. It can certainly be painful and uncomfortable. When we don't yet know (or we forget) that this aching feeling is also soulful and beautiful, we may try to satisfy our longing in unhelpful ways. Our natural and precious longing can become subsumed by consumerism; the desire for the next and better possession, the desire for fame and riches. Of course, these drives are natural and serve us well in many ways. We need tangible and intangible things to survive and to live a fulfilling and rewarding life. Possessions can give us a great deal of pleasure and delight—and they certainly can be soulful. They are also the basis for creating economic abundance and other important social structures. However, the drive for more and more can take us so far away from stillness we no longer recognise our longing or can bear to be with it long enough for it to teach us. Addiction can be another way of responding to our natural longing, but in a very destructive way. Our natural and sweet longing for the experience of wholeness will then be swamped by the brutal experience of craving.

Divine longing is not craving or desire. The more you experience craving and desire the more agitated you tend to become, whereas longing is stilling and deepening. It may be painful, there may be a deep ache to it, but it is life-giving. It gives rise to love and to a fullness of heart. The tears that come from longing are sweet and purifying. They can be painful and they are filled with sacredness. They undo us and leave us feeling humble, open and soft. They unmask all the schemes and manoeuvres we may have come up with to satisfy a desire or craving, or impress someone. They invite us deeper into ourselves.

It is important to recognise that while our fleeting desires for something pleasant, or for something that tastes or smells good or flatters us, may also be natural, they are shadows of our deepest longing. We do need to be wise and practical in what we think these experiences will give us. If we think they are going to satisfy the sacred longing we have for the experience of oneness with our own being, we are naturally going to be disappointed in time. Sometimes our longing remains present even when the very thing we thought we wanted is right there with us. Seventeenth-century Japanese poet Basho captures this so beautifully when he writes: 'Even in Kyoto, hearing the cuckoo's cry, I long for Kyoto.'

LONGING FOR MY TRUE HOME—RUBY

I remember once driving down our dirt road, feeling quite sad and blue. I asked myself what the matter was. Even though I had been living in a different country for over ten years by then, my first thought was, 'I think I'm homesick for my country.' But then I thought 'No, that's not it. It's Mum I'm missing.' You see, I had not seen my mother for over a year. Then I thought, 'You know, I *am* missing my country and I *am* missing my mother, but that is not it. What am I really homesick for?' Then, in a flash, the surprising answer came. I realised that, actually, it is myself I am missing. With three children under five I fall in a heap of exhaustion every night. I don't have time to scratch myself. I have not had time to just sit quietly and be in my own company; figure out what I am thinking and feeling; just hear my own wheels turning. Yes, I am missing my own internal presence.

There was something really lovely and calming about recognising that longing for what it was. The sadness was still there and I didn't know what I was going to be able to do about it, but it got all soft and sweet at that moment. Amazingly, just realising that I was missing myself gave me the feeling of being with myself.

There is a sacred yearning, a longing inside. It is the soul's desire to go home, to be recognised and to fulfil its destiny. It calls us forward to places, paths and peers—people who we feel are our true tribe. It also calls us towards expressing our talents and creativity and wholeheartedly performing our work in the world. It is life longing for itself.

CREATIVITY CALLING—VELMA

Today I am bored and sad and I'm having flashes of anger towards my partner who is so tired and drained he is not present or pleasant. But in my stomach something is calling. What? A small circle of energy, a small swirl of energy beckons me. Is it my long-ignored creativity that is calling me? It wants me to create something, make something, do something, decide something. But what? It won't solidify and take a shape. It's not ready to reveal itself. It just wants to swirl and beat like a heart.

In our society we often do not recognise this longing for what it is; we think it is unhappiness or depression or boredom. We think we have have to find an outlet or a 'solution' for it as soon as possible. But what if we simply stayed with the feeling of longing until it revealed itself more fully? What might we find? It seems to me that if you sit long enough and kindly enough with *any* feeling, it transforms into longing. And if you sit long enough with longing, you see that you could accurately call it Love. Unfortunately, we rarely call it that and often try to answer that vague feeling of dissatisfaction with possessions, actions and busy-ness. But it can never be shackled to things and actions in that way.

SPREADING OUT—HELENE

I remember a Sunday evening when I was about 11 or 12. My parents decided that everyone was going to bed early. As I clomped around angrily getting ready for bed I suddenly felt interminably bored. The blandness of this flat, suburban reality filled me with longing. I wanted something to be happening, but what? I couldn't think of *anything* that could possibly be enough to fill up the void. Mum saw my annoyance and came and sat on my bed. She said, 'If there is anything you need to tell me, you can always come and talk to me.' I knew she meant boys; something I'd done and felt guilty about, something she could put a stop to. I let her think by my continued silence that maybe there was something. I couldn't admit to what I was actually feeling because I could not begin to put it into words, and I thought I had no right to feel it: the horror of endless flatness and longing.

I've spent years avoiding that space, that dark cavern that looms open like a gap in the earth's crust. Now, in moments, I peer in, I go into it, down further and further into it. Then sometimes the black endless space reveals another side to itself—a kind of peace, an endless infinity that testifies to the impermanence of me as an individual; the vast empty plain in which no form can be sustained. No entertainment, thought, fantasy, life story, book, toy—no matter how engrossing or even inspiring—will bring complete and lasting satisfaction. Truly accepting this for a moment, I spread out into that vastness and experience its gentle spaciousness where boredom and sadness become peace and breathing. Nothing else, just breathing.

Mahatma Gandhi spoke about 'blessed monotony'; another spiritual leader, Chogyam Trungpa, said that if you stare at it long enough, eventually agitated boredom becomes cool and spacious boredom. He spoke of how boredom can play a role in 'destroying credentials'—helping us shed all the grand and inflated ideas we have about our self-importance. In the same way we don't want to use our sadness to create credentials either. It's not helpful to create an identity out of sadness, using it like a dark cloak of magnificent melancholy to add another bit of drama to our life story. Instead, we can let it pare us down and take us into the bedrock of who we really are. Strangely, joy arises as we let go of the struggle and surrender to the state of soulful sadness and the longing that exists within it.

It takes courage to be with our longing. It requires space and time to attend soulfully to sadness. In fact, reflection can be seen as a key feature of soulfulness. We will return to this theme of releasing busy-ness and creating space for reflection over and over as we travel through the cycle of soulful sadness.

When our experience of longing breaks free of objects, we find ourselves not so much longing *for* something, but gently simmering in the experience of pure bitter-sweet longing itself. We can experience how the very acknowledgement and honouring of longing sweetens the moment and works its transmutation in us—becoming its own reward.

LONGING FOR WINGS—FRANCINE

One day my four-year-old discovered that one of her teeth had become a little bit wobbly. It was a long-awaited event and as she worked it a little looser she began to anticipate the visit of the tooth fairy. She had been told that the tooth fairy would leave her some money in exchange for her tooth. This was the problem, you see. Money is okay as far as it goes, but what she really longed

for was something far more important, far more magical, far more archetypal: she wanted to be able to fly. She asked me if I could do a deal with the tooth fairy on her behalf, where the money gets exchanged for flying lessons.
I cast around at lightning speed for a way to soften one of life's great disappointments: humans can't fly.

'But you can fly in your dreams, can't you?' I asked. 'Yes,' she said, 'but I really want to be able to fly when I'm awake.' My heart broke a little. I knew it would take a very long time, perhaps her whole life, to become light enough or awake enough to fly that way.

Sometimes, we think we are experiencing sadness when it is actually a deep, deep call from within. We think it is loneliness, we think it is depression, when it is longing, it is yearning—and it's sweet.

Stop and sit with it.

Let everything to do with sadness, all the nuances—the disappointment, the feeling of being slightly out of sorts, the vague agitation, that slight ache, that gravitational pull, that . . . I don't know
. . . what is it? . . . sacred longing—let it pull you inside. Hear that deep call of the soul. Hold it gently inside and it will work its smouldering magic and bring about transformation.

CHAPTER 5

ENTERING LIMINAL SPACE—NOT KNOWING

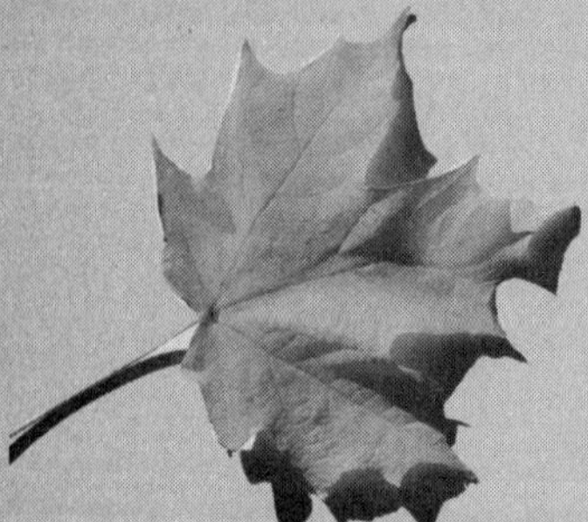

CHAPTER FIVE

'What do I do next?'
'What decision should I make?'
'Should I leave my job?'
'How can I help my son?'
'Will she pull through?'
'Should I stay in this relationship?'

'I don't know.'

We have arrived at the second doorway in the cycle of soulful sadness—the 'liminal' place of not knowing. At this point, we have to admit we have no answers. We truly don't know. We don't know the way forward, the way back, or even how we got here. We are in between. Suspended.

In the first phase of the cycle we felt the longing of the soul calling us . . . calling us to . . . calling us to . . . we're not quite sure. We felt a subtle yet powerful tug within like the pull of the moon on the tides, but we don't quite know where it's leading us or what we are meant to 'do' with it. We really don't know if everything will work out or not. Our pat answers and formulas don't seem adequate. We want to abandon them. Our old solutions no longer seem to hold water but there aren't any new ones to put in their place. We don't know what decision to make, what the key to our situation is. Everything may seem slightly tinged with failure—even the roaring successes. Sounding very like Winnie-the-Pooh's chronically melancholy friend Eyore, we are tempted to say, 'I give up', 'What's the point?', 'Is change really possible?' and 'How very like life to bring me here once again.'

We may feel annoyed or uncomfortable with the experience of 'I don't know'. Many of us think we *should* know and we may feel embarrassed, frustrated or inadequate when we don't.

Not knowing has a certain fire that can be hard to bear. However, as we learn to become more familiar with liminal space, our frustration and fear dissipate and sometimes we can even laugh as we catch our plans and strategies once again coming unstuck. Suddenly, we lose all our bluster like a balloon deflating. Our body language changes, the shoulders deflate a little, and we may even feel a bit of self-pity. But, as we notice what is happening with a compassionate eye and surrender to liminal space, our posture changes and we aren't feeling sorry for ourselves anymore; we simply don't know. And that's alright!

In this phase of the cycle of soulful sadness we are invited to sigh, to let go into the experience and to simply sit in not knowing. We let go of thrashing around and clawing for a solution, and just wait. We are asked to remain in this in-between space where deciding, planning and scheming have no place. In this phase of the cycle it is best not to busily consult others, to resist the temptation to think that someone else has the perfect answer or a magic-bullet solution for us.

This not knowing can be mournful, wistful, tinged with unfathomable sadness and even grieving. It may feel like a painful simmer of recognition that once again we are undone. We cook in this. We recognise that our own effort alone does not suffice, and paradoxically this is a relief. We may see that for quite a while before the cycle of soulful sadness began we were holding our breath with strain. We were waiting to exhale. As we enter liminal space we may find ourselves sighing deeply and breathing out with the sweet relief of letting go.

The second phase in the cycle of soulful sadness teaches us to deflate through the humbling experience of not knowing. When we open to liminal space in this way it can touch us softly like mist or dew. As we sit quietly in this phase, we are not spraying our emotions around, so we feel more contained. One person said to me, 'It does feel a bit sad but it also feels sane.' It may be tinged with aloneness, but it is not lonely or bereft.

TEN THINGS I DON'T KNOW

Make a list of ten things you don't know by completing this sentence starter: 'I don't know . . . ' You might find it useful to add 'what', 'how', 'when', 'whether' or 'if' onto the end of the sentence starter (I don't know *how* . . . *if* . . .

etc.). You may want to sweep through some broad subject areas such as science, economics, sport, cookery, car maintenance, relationships or geography. Nothing is out of bounds. Let your sense of humour come into play—some of the things you list may be flippant and fun, some may be profound and meaningful, some unexpected and out of left field. Have fun creating a list containing simple, complex and whacky things you don't know.

You may wish to try this with friends as a light-hearted exercise, party game or dinner activity; it can be delightful, meaningful and even hilarious to hear each other's lists. Once you have your list of ten things you don't know, read it out loud to the group or silently to yourself.

These are things you simply don't know at this time. One day you may know something about some of these things. Some of them you may never know, or never *want* to know. For now, enjoy the feeling of simply not knowing. Take some time to breathe deeply and relax into the feeling that it is okay to not know these things at this time.

Here are some examples of lists.

Celia's 'I don't know. . .
- how the planets move;
- where south is;
- why small hands and sloping shoulders turn me off;
- how the economy works;
- how to speak Swahili;
- what happens when you die;
- what I'm supposed to be doing with my life;
- why he makes me so nervous;
- anything about the Theory of Relativity; or
- if people can really change.'

> **Josh's 'I don't know . . .**
> - how electricity works;
> - why people can't get on;
> - how to divide fractions;
> - the population of Belgium;
> - how to spell 'onamatapaya' — or do I? [Don't think so, Josh.]
> - where love comes from;
> - how preferences work in an election;
> - what a soufflé is;
> - why ships that weigh thousands of tonnes don't sink; or
> - how to play chess.'

There can be a feeling of freedom in acknowledging that there are many things that remain a puzzle to us. Often it is so much more fruitful to connect with the sheer mystery of the way things are rather than claim to know them and explain them to others.

Have you noticed that sometimes 'knowing' can be very destructive — like fundamentalists who 'know' that their belief system is right and others are wrong. How much violence has this kind of knowing been responsible for? How freeing it can be for ourselves and others when we don't know! It allows for other possibilities to emerge and it helps us develop empathy and connection with others.

HOW COME THEY DON'T KNOW?—MOLLY

Before I had children I used to watch mothers with unruly children in the supermarket and look down my nose at their parenting skills, sniffing at the bright-coloured fizzy drink that might be in their trolleys, thinking, 'How come they don't seem to know how parenting should be done?'

Then I had kids of my own and my two-year-old took up the habit of outstretching both arms as we went down the rows of the supermarket, having a tactile experience with as many packages on both sides of the aisle as possible. This, and other daily humiliations such as 'arsenic hour' (the constant fussing and crying at 5.00 every afternoon) meant that I stopped finding fault with other mothers and simply wanted to offer to help when I saw them struggling.

The experience of soulful sadness awakens you to a compassionate connection with others by challenging what you think you know and deflating your judgement of others. It invites you to put yourself in another's shoes, even if their life seems very far removed from your own.

For most of us, sadness is uncomfortable and our knee-jerk reaction is to try to make it go away as quickly as possible. So we try to jump to a 'solution' to the problem. Solutions are good; more than good, they are great! But we must be wary of grasping for them too soon. We are complex creatures and many of our difficulties, such as those within relationships, cannot be neatly solved. Sometimes the most effective solution may be quite unexpected and seemingly unconnected to the problem. For example, a fresh coat of paint in the office can have a surprisingly positive effect on strained relationships. So, responding to our feelings of sadness by sitting in not knowing for a time can leave space for surprising and serendipitous solutions to emerge.

It is such a relief to realise that we don't always have to know everything or make decisions. We can feel so bogged down and 'heavy' trying to reach a solution or a decision when they are simply not ready to emerge.

In fact, at times of significant transitions (liminal phases), such as when newly retired or bereaved, it is better *not* to make major decisions. This is the cardinal rule presented in retirement seminars: don't pack up the cat and move to Brazil the day after you are handed the gold watch—wait until the liminal phase of transition has had time to mature.

Another reason to wait before jumping to a solution is that if you think you know, you tend to see only what you already know. You may not be prepared to look with completely open eyes. Or you may look but see nothing at all. When something is completely outside your realm of knowledge you may claim that nothing is there even if it is right under your nose.

When Europeans first came to Australia they described it as *terra nullius*, a Latin term meaning 'empty country'. They did not recognise the legitimate presence of the people who had occupied the land for thousands of years. It is easy to be incredulous and to point the finger about this, but it is sobering to see how much this tendency is at play in our own lives.

TERRA NULLIUS—BETH

When we first moved from the city to the country, I thought that a lot of the land around our property at the end of a dirt road was *terra nullius*. I would go for a walk up the bush track behind our house and it seemed to me that nobody occupied or cared about that land. To me, it was left over from the gold rush days, slowly being reclaimed by the eucalypts, coffee bushes and kangaroos. Local people spoke of that area as beautiful, but the truth is, I could not see any beauty in it for a long time. To me it simply looked abandoned and sad.

Time passed and I walked there a lot, through all the different seasons. I began to notice when saplings had been planted and fences repaired. One day I met a local farmer on the bush track and he told me bits and pieces about the land—who built which fence, when the bee hives arrived and how old Bob had put the firebreak in.

Even though much of this land is scarred by mining, people have cared about it for thousands of years. The current owners know when someone takes a sapling for a Christmas tree or rides a horse through there. The more I walked there the more I could see that this area is not just known and watched over by humans, but it is also a kangaroo sleeping ground and home to countless other creatures, insects and birds. In high summer the bush crackles as the eucalypt oil snaps in the heat and cicadas shrill at 120 decibels, approaching the threshold of human pain.

And there seems to be something else hanging behind the heat and the cold too, an ancient presence that many people call the spirit of the land. So, it is definitely not *terra nullius*.

Soulful sadness can be like this story. With just a superficial glance we may say, 'There is nothing here for me.' But it may not be what we first think it is. We may need to suspend our judgement of it so that we can invite a new vision of our experience to emerge. We may need to spend some time just being in the landscape of our soulful sadness and observing it, so that we can begin to see what really inhabits that territory.

The word 'liminal' is derived from *limen*, a Latin word meaning 'threshold'. So the experience of liminal space indicates a threshold or a time of transition. We are not where we were, but we have not yet arrived at our destination either. People sometimes speak of feeling a burden lifting at these times—neither the past nor the future are occupying our attention, so we are free to enter the present moment more fully—and even if we feel alone, the present is a powerful place to be because that is where change takes place.

Our architecture and landscape are filled with liminal places. Archways, doors, windows, lifts, verandahs, airports, springs, marshes, caves, motels, roadhouses, waiting rooms, boom gates, canals, piers, rivers, dams, mountain passes, crossroads and bridges are all liminal places in the landscape. These places can be strangely comforting when we ourselves are in a liminal phase. Even though we may think of roadhouses and railway cafés as unattractive places with their fluorescent lights and plastic chairs, sometimes the anonymous comings and goings of strangers seems to support our solitary journey in liminal space. We could even experiment with deliberately going to such places when we feel ourselves entering this phase of soulful sadness.

I know a writer who sometimes goes to the airport, sits in a chair and jots things down in a notebook as he watches people coming and going. He says he finds stories arising in his mind about who the people are, where they are going and why. Perhaps a liminal space where strangers are coming and going frees the quiet observer to create and dream. Similarly, being on a ferry, a train or a plane can be very centring. Perhaps this is one of the reasons why travel pleases so many people. We become quiet inside and enjoy the feeling of freedom that arises from not being where we left but not being where we are going either; for a time we are released from the past and the future, and held in the liminal present.

BRINGING HER HOME—TAI

Recently I returned to the city where I grew up, and walked through the streets of my childhood in what became clear was a 'retrieval' of the fragmented parts of myself as well as those aspects of me that had found joy and solace in my past. I wandered through many parks and greeted old friends: creeks and grandmother trees, rocks and paths that I had skipped and played and ruminated on in the past. I found that I crossed many bridges—literal ones—in my wanderings and stopped on a particular bridge made from large, round stones with a beautiful curve to it. This solid structure seemed to almost move with me as I walked across it. I sat on this bridge in total awe and bewilderment at how I loved to be there, how delicious it was to simply be there.

A few weeks later when I heard about 'liminal spaces' I knew that I had gone to the bridges, the creeks and the trees of my childhood and picked up an aspect of myself that was a little girl waiting there, in between dimensions and spaces, still dreaming, still full of hope and wonder, still looking for me. I took her hand and brought her home with me.

> ### VISITING A LIMINAL PLACE
> Choose a liminal place near you. Perhaps a café, a bridge, an airport, a waiting lounge in a train station, a pathway between two places, a hotel lobby, a leafy garden arbour. If you prefer to experience this at home, go to your balcony or verandah or place a chair directly under a door frame.
>
> Go there and absorb the feeling of the space. Experience how you are freed to just observe when you are in a liminal place. In the privacy of your mind you may wish to briefly salute the past, and touch lightly on the empty space of the future, and then settle here in the space between them both. Take in the sounds of clinking cutlery, people walking, children playing in the distance. If you are at an airport, enjoy that you are not queuing at the check-in, or rifling through your pockets for passports, tickets or timetables. Watch the ebb and flow of traffic. Sometimes there is a crush of bustling people, then it empties and becomes still for a while. Just be here in this liminal space. No conclusions to reach, no plans to make, nothing to solve. For now, you don't know, and you can experience the subtle release of a liminal place. Linger there in silence for a while and then leave when it's time.

The idea of 'liminal' space or activities was first brought into the public arena by anthropologists such as Victor Turner while studying the rites of passage of indigenous peoples. He described liminal ceremonies such as initiations and noted that these important transitions in a person's life mark their passage into a new identity and greater status. He also noted that these powerful ceremonies often contain elements of danger. We can see similar elements of liminal space at play in modern Western ceremonies, such as graduations, engagements, marriages, christenings and funerals. And some, like initiations into fraternities, can spill over into dangerous territory when they are not overseen by responsible elders.

Even stages of life, such as the teenage years, can be seen as liminal. These are the in-between years when childhood has been left behind but adulthood has not yet arrived. A teenager can undergo dramatic changes in identity and parents do sometimes feel that it's all a bit edgy and dangerous. A teen's identity can shape-shift at the drop of a hat; you look up and your teen is a goth, then an environmental activist, then a nocturnal poet and recluse. Even in the midst of something very familiar, you can wake up one morning to feel you do not know it at all!

States of consciousness too can be seen as liminal, such as when just waking up, when meditating, sleepwalking, or suspended in a coma. There are liminal times of the day like daybreak or twilight, or of the calendar like New Year's Eve and birthdays, or one-off occasions, like childbirth. Periods of retreat or fasting can be seen as liminal experiences. Cleansing, detoxing and vision-questing—forty days and nights in the desert, so to speak—can also be thought of as liminal experiences. Objects can have liminal qualities as well, such as a pendulum when it is suspended in between the up and down swing. A powerful sense of infinity can be felt in that tiny liminal moment of suspension.

There are also liminal physical states, such as pregnancy, childbirth and menstruation. The recent work of authors like Jane Bennett and Alexandra Pope draws our attention to the liminal opportunity that menstruation offers. This research is playing a part in recovering ancient knowledge about menstruation as a liminal time for stepping out of the day-to-day hustle—a gateway for women to experience the joy of communing with female wisdom. Rather than seeing menstruation as a time of limitation filled with cramps and bad moods, we can come to know it as a powerful time for becoming still and gathering the wisdom that can open up at these times.

Sometimes during times of sadness we have liminal dreams. Any dream that includes a difficult attempt to lift off or get somewhere can be an indication of a period of transition where the old is no longer serving but the new has yet to emerge. I remember one dream in which I was crossing a busy highway in a daze only to get to the middle and realise I couldn't go back or forward. Other liminal dream images can include boats, trains, or that hoary old classic—trying to get to the airport to catch a flight only to find you have to return home because you've forgotten your passport.

There is tremendous potential in liminal states because they are times when former identities are dissolved so that something new can unfold. But liminal states are best when they are temporary; when they go on for too long they can become destructive. Think of refugees who are held in limbo without visas, people who are placed under house arrest indefinitely, those in hiding from persecution or in gaol, and those who are forced to wait year after year for news of a missing loved one. Many migrants live with an undercurrent of liminal sadness; they feel they no longer belong in their birth country but do not fully belong in their adoptive country either.

For a variety of reasons people can go through years of living with an almost constant sense of being suspended betwixt and between, especially if the sadness is caused by very deep trauma and grief. Even when there does not seem to be any reason for it, some people have this experience of being caught in the 'land of not belonging' and it can become a defining flavour of that person's soul—almost as if they carry liminal space with them as a lifelong companion. It is such a mystery of the soul that it seeks out such companions, don't you think? But sometimes it does, and this is its own wisdom. After prolonged and deep contemplation some people learn to transmute the pain of this in such a way that it becomes a teacher for them rather than a random and cruel persecutor.

The value of the temporary timeframe holds true for all the phases of soulful sadness. It is best to visit them for a time before going on to the next phase when you are moved to do so. If you become stuck in any one of the phases for too long I believe you can freeze into depression. To me, this is one of the most useful aspects of becoming aware of the cycle of soulful sadness: if you have an idea about what the next phase may be you can more skilfully facilitate yourself to step into it when you feel the time is right. Most often the transition to the next phase happens naturally; you don't have to worry about it or do anything to make it happen—it simply unfolds from your conscious engagement with the phase before. However, if you find yourself getting stuck and you intuitively know it is no longer useful for you to be there, you can invite yourself to move on by simply reflecting on the next phase and trying some of the activities that belong with that phase. Of course, when you are bogged down and really struggling with sadness, you should not hesitate to seek professional help.

While prolonged and painful experiences of liminal space belong to the realms of deep grieving, you are much more likely to find yourself in the liminal phase of not knowing for a couple of weeks, several days, a single day or perhaps just an hour. Once you give yourself permission to relax there, the liminal space of not knowing can be a cooling and spacious place to be. When you think about it, you will see how your heart and mind already court liminal space. The thought of a daytime nap can be so captivating and delicious. A gap year, a sabbatical, a day off school or work can be essential times of liminal pause. I have a friend who is a father of four and a graphic designer working from home. He declares a 'mental health day' every once in a while and on this day he refuses to get out of his pyjamas, turn on his computer, answer the phone or do any chores. Also, the time-honoured cure of taking to one's bed for a whole day can be a delightful way of releasing the burdens of busy-ness and entering a healing liminal space—the bed is a boat floating in the liminal ocean of the bedroom.

Sometimes the liminal phase of 'not knowing' may feel frustrating and boring—especially towards the end of the phase. You want your new life to begin, but it may not be ready. A chrysalis has to develop and it won't survive if little fingers probe and push it to hurry up. Gestation has to be respected, so it is useful to allow the liminal phase of soulful sadness the spaciousness it needs. This means resisting the temptation to jump to solutions or fill up every second with activity.

It may feel like nothing is happening when you are in the liminal phase of soulful sadness, but it isn't necessarily so. It is a time for lying fallow and gathering strength. It is a time of internal ripening and cooking. If you do not run away from not knowing, if you just stay in the mystery, the difficulty or even the boredom of it, if you simply stand in humility and are not tossed away, then something opens up. You penetrate the superficial skin of not knowing and experience the vast spaciousness beneath it. As you simply stay and endure, it is as if each moment loosens and reveals itself. It may not seem very glamorous, it may even seem masochistic and old fashioned, but even a small dose of patience and containment in the face of sadness and not knowing can lead to unexpected richness.

Have you ever watched a sheepdog holding and containing a herd of sheep? The dog is totally still, every inch of its body present, holding and holding, waiting for the command—this is the suspended animation of liminal space. In a similar way, but perhaps with a little more relaxation than the sheepdog, we can develop steadiness by holding in not knowing, while staying alert to the stirrings of the next phase of the cycle when it is ready to unfold.

Through the cycle of soulful sadness a kind of positive dissolution happens as things we thought we knew and who we thought we were melt away. This is the necessary unplugging of our fixed and limited identity so that something much more fluid, expanded and loving can emerge. This transformation is described over and over again in the biographies of mystics and seekers from centuries ago as well as those who walk among us today. Each one brings their own character to the experience of the dissolution of what they thought they knew—some go kicking and screaming, and others sighing, dancing and laughing, but go they do—and so do we.

While the 'not knowing' that we experience as part of our journey through soulful sadness may not be the full extent of that radical realignment, it is tinged with the same quality and holds a little of this same promise. Something old in us can be shed and something new can be nurtured through sitting still in the uncertainty of liminal space.

THE FIRE OF NOT KNOWING—KAZ

One day we received a letter under the door. It was a notice from the council saying that the water in the street would be turned off for a couple of hours for repairs. A friend was due to visit that day so I filled the bath with water to tide us over and cleaned the house in preparation for her arrival. When I'd finished, I bundled my baby into his pram and walked to the train station to meet her. Something must have come up because she wasn't on the train, so I decided to walk back home. I rounded the corner only to find a neighbour running towards me screaming, 'Your house is on fire!' With no water available for garden hoses, I watched as our house was almost completely consumed in the 12 minutes it took for the fire brigade to arrive.

In the following weeks and months, I tried to make sense of what had happened. Why? Surely there had to be a reason? What was this painful experience all about? I kept trying to understand it, see signs, get messages that would clarify the 'why' of it all.

One evening I was meditating and once again I was trying to fathom this very painful experience. Into the stillness I asked, 'What am I meant to understand or learn from this?' As if in response to my sincere question, the thought arose: 'If I held your hand all the way and told you *it's okay, it's okay*, and gave you a clear explanation of why so it all made perfect sense to you, what would you really be able to offer of yourself?'

This was not a solution or an explanation but for the first time it dawned on me that *not* knowing can have its own transformative power. It is when I am groping in the dark, when I am not even sure anything makes any sense at all and yet I am still somehow, clumsily, able to offer myself to the fire of life, that real transformation can take place. In that moment, with the searing awareness of the value of not knowing, there was a feeling of sweet surrender accompanied by the relief that comes with the hint of humility. This insight sustained me many, many times as the fallout from the fire continued to reverberate in our lives.

St John of the Cross, a sixteenth-century Spanish Christian mystic, wrote of *la noche oscura*, which is often translated as 'the dark night of the soul' and is thought of by many as a time of deep sadness. But author and scholar Gerald May points out that a better translation of *oscura* is actually 'obscure', 'not known' or 'hidden'. John's spiritual writings encapsulate the understanding that for a time—sometimes a painful and confusing time—we do not know, and it is *right* that we do not know.

This is because powerfully transformative processes are at play and if we thought we knew what should happen next we would try to direct the process and derail what actually needs to emerge. When we think we know exactly where we are going and why and what every step should be, we can easily get in the way. In not knowing we are open to entirely unexpected possibilities and pathways. According to St John the real purpose of the Dark Night or the Night of Not Knowing is a deepening of love and trust, and this can only be brought about with a loosening of the ego.

> **SHOWER POWER**
>
> Take a shower and as you let the water fall over your body imagine that all your concepts about what you know, your judgements about success and failure and all the 'shoulds' you may have accumulated along the way, are flowing away with the water and that, in their place, trust and love are arising. Imagine.

Liminal space—the sense of not knowing with certainty—is part of the deepening power of soulful sadness. It is through allowing, and even embracing, this uncertainty that soulful sadness teaches us. For a time we need to bear the fire of not knowing. It helps us put aside all our pat answers and become more humble. We need this humility so that we can learn to listen and notice the clues that are all around us. We may stumble around in the dark for a while, but gradually our eyes will adjust; we will gather some night vision and begin to notice a way forward. This is so much more fruitful than leaping to a fragile and ego-generated bluster of certainty about how things are and how things should be. So there is no shame when we find ourselves undone as soulful melancholy comes along, bringing us its gift of uncertainty. Even a few minutes of true humility in not knowing can shift us powerfully into the territory of the next phase—deep listening.

CHAPTER 6

ATTENDING TO STILLNESS—DEEP LISTENING

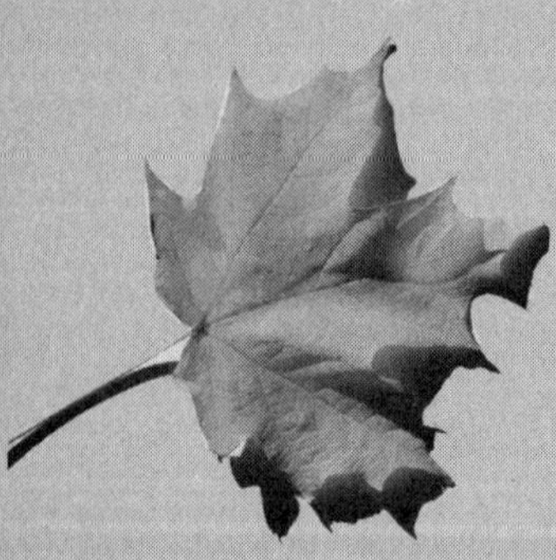

CHAPTER SIX

As we sit in the liminal phase of not knowing, we begin to wind down and eventually, to notice the presence of stillness. The more we listen, the stiller we become, and somehow the longing that drew us into the cycle of soulful melancholy begins to sweeten. With the humility that arises in the liminal space of not knowing, our pat answers fall away and we want to attend more carefully to each moment. Because, we are now more inclined to listen, and learning becomes more available to us. We are drawn to watch things more carefully and pay attention to people when they speak. We have entered the third phase in the cycle of soulful sadness—'Attending to Stillness'—where deep listening is called for.

In the first phase of the cycle the call of the soul put us in touch with our own longing, and our time in the second phase of liminal space invited us to admit that we don't know. In this third phase the longing sweetens and deepens into stillness. For this precious window of time we have become humble enough to truly listen and we begin to become receptive. Instead of giving our attention to what it is we are feeling, we want to listen. We become still and focused like a deer that stops in its tracks and listens intently for the slightest rustle of the leaves. In the first phase of the cycle our soul has sent out a call in the form of our longing and now we begin to listen for a faint reply from way across the valley.

Most people find that during a time of soulful sadness social events lose their allure. It may take you a while to realise what is happening, but by the third phase, 'Attending to Stillness', you may find youself making active choices about what you will, and will not, do.

OUT OF LIMINAL SPACE, STILLNESS ARISES—LEE

Sometimes it takes me a while to slow down and realise that I feel sad. Then I become very quiet and sometimes tearful. After a while I begin to sense the stillness beneath the sadness. At first the stillness itself seems to be tinged with soft grief. It's sad but also quite beautiful in its own way.

Then a shift happens: as the stillness takes up more of my attention, the tears end and something other than me begins to fill my awareness. Subtly, my sad drama slowly fades from the centre of the stage—I am no longer so fully aware of *me* feeling the disappointment, *me* aching with longing, *me* doing the waiting, *me* not knowing. My focus shifts away from my own immediate experience and I begin to listen *beyond* my thoughts and feelings. This internal shift in the direction of my attention signals that the liminal phase has drawn to a close and I am entering the next phase: 'Attending to Stillness—Deep Listening'.

I notice the throb of my blood in my ears. I hear my breath coming in and going out. I fall into the sounds of silence; the creaking of the house, the sound of traffic in the distance. I fall into quiet daydreams in random places, at random moments. I linger in the car even after parking it. I feel drawn to read poetry, write in my journal, listen to specific music, lie on my bedroom floor at night in the dark, light a candle, stare at the fire. I am slow to return phone calls, slow to answer questions—much slower at doing anything, really. I am in retreat.

By now you may have realised that this is a time to scale back on social activities or find other ways to meet important social obligations such as putting in only a brief appearance, rescheduling altogether or choosing more restful settings for meeting others. Without alarming anyone or dramatising the situation, simply seek out alone times. While pottering in the quiet of your own company you may find yourself sitting and staring into space every now and then. While alone at home in the quiet of the house you may notice things you don't ordinarily notice, such as the vibration of the electrical mains, or dust motes drifting in a shaft of light, or the way a sitting cat will sway ever so slightly back and forth as she breathes.

Sometimes people become afraid of this pull to be alone and they worry that they may permanently lose the desire or the ability to socialise. Some say this pull towards stillness and aloneness is painful—but aloneness is not loneliness. I believe these fears about being alone come about largely because most of us are not taught to value quiet alone times, so we have no way of interpreting this pull towards retreat, except to describe it as frightening, painful or lonely. But is it really? Next time you feel this pull towards quiet retreat, why not welcome it, spend time really feeling out the nature and quality of it? You may discover that it can be trusted as a mood of the soul and that it is wistfully sweet. If you go with the pull towards aloneness, it will naturally release you when the time comes and you will be drawn to engage with the company of others once again, bringing the flavour of stillness with you.

While it may be scary at first to acknowledge and to act on the pull towards our own company, in the end it is much more painful to try to mask it with lots of noise and social interaction. When we are feeling the presence of sadness and we want it to open into a soulful experience, a noisy party can jangle our exposed nerves and contrast very painfully with our mood. Paradoxically, feelings of alienation and isolation can intensify easily in crowded situations. The extroverted company of others is not what serves us best at this time and we are likely to be far more consoled by activities such as lying on the bedroom floor and following our breath coming in and going out. As we do so, we may be reminded of the seasons and the endless movement of waves on the sand. It is as if we are stopping to listen for the heartbeat of the earth, entering the present moment more fully and calling our thoughts home like birds coming in to roost for the night.

THE BIG NIGHT IN

Plan an hour or two alone at home during the evening for a 'listening date' with yourself. There are a few things you will need to do to prepare. Borrow or buy a small bell or gong with a pleasant sound. Select some quiet music, a book of poems, quotations, paintings or photographs. There is only one criteria for what you select: you must find it beautiful and stilling. Browse your local library for books and music if you do not have anything suitable. Prepare your 'listening space' so that it is clean and uncluttered. Turn off your phone, unplug the TV, shut down your computer. If you wish, subdue the lighting. If you do not have a dimmer switch, you can place a scarf over a lamp, or light some candles. Prepare a warm beverage or water. Take a shower, dress in comfortable clothes, moisturise your skin and, if you like, dab on some fragrant oil or perfume.

Sit in a comfortable chair or lie down on your back and listen. Rub your ears and then your face gently with your open palms and listen to the sound. Ring the bell or strike the gong gently. Listen very consciously to the sound. See if you can follow the sound as it fades and fades, right to the point when it becomes inaudible and beyond. You may want to do this several times. Now be aware of all the sounds outside, in the room and inside you. Can you hear your eyelids blinking? Your heart beating? Notice your breathing as you lie or sit and listen.

Making all your movements slow and fluid, turn on your music. While you are listening to the music you may want to slowly turn the pages of your book, reading a line or two, or looking at the images. Be aware of the sound of your clothes rustling as you move. If you have a pot of tea or jug of water beside you, be aware of the sound as you pour and slowly swallow. Pause every now and then to listen to the music and let it fill your ears and your whole body with sound. As the music or your slow page-turning ends, listen once more into the silence. Nothing to do. You are not trying to make yourself hear anything—you are just quietly listening.

The inclination to listen arises naturally when you have been though a liminal space and realise that you truly don't know. So during this third phase in the cycle of soulful sadness you may find yourself wanting to hone your capacity to listen to others, to listen to yourself and to listen beyond yourself into the 'Great Silence' (the Divine, the Immensity—or whatever words you feel comfortable using). These three directions of listening go hand in hand and you could say that at their deepest level they are one and the same thing.

NEWS FROM HOME—NICK

I woke up with the thought that I would like to improve my listening habits. Not because 'better listening skills' would be a tasty notch on my belt, but because people are worth listening to.

What is listening, I wondered? To listen well, I need to hear the words *and* feel what is behind the words. For this, humility is required; without humility listening fully is not possible. When I'm listening while thinking about what I'm going to say next, I'm really only having a conversation with my ego; I'm listening from a place where I'm the main character in the story. This is not really listening.

I think the essence of listening is 'being a witness to', being fully present while someone puts their point of view, expresses how they feel or tells a story from their life. The listener remains focused on the other person. The speaker knows they are being heard with respect and so their story has a safe place to land. This is a very powerful experience for the listener and the speaker.

It's easy for me to be the one talking; it's much harder to be the one listening. To me really listening is a prayer; not prayer in the sense of asking or petitioning, but prayer in the sense of receptivity, emptiness and being a vessel. I've noticed that when I'm able to do anything from a place of true listening, it becomes letters from a deep source, news from home.

To listen to others well we have to understand that people are not there simply for our benefit. This sounds obvious but it is a difficult thing to truly wake up to and can be especially remote when we are sad, because sadness can consume us and cut us off from the capacity to step outside our own reality. For sadness to become soulful we have to learn the knack of letting it touch us in ways that open us—to ourselves and others—rather than closing us off in fright.

By listening to another person with undivided attention both people receive a gift. The listener is uplifted by the experience of giving their respect and benefits from the other person's perspective. The speaker receives the healing power of being heard and acknowledged. The listener provides a safe place for the speaker's story to land, and both are enriched by the subtle connection that is then formed between them.

In the presence of pain and sadness often the most important thing is to be heard rather than to be offered solutions, explanations, excuses or suggestions. Respectful listening creates an atmosphere of trust where each person's own wisdom is called forth. The power of listening rests on the listener's capacity to give their focus to the speaker rather than

trying to capture the focus of the conversation for themselves. This can be hard to do for many of us! We may think we don't hijack the agenda when listening to others, but it is really sobering to see how subtle and recurring that impulse can be.

Especially when we are listening to someone who is sad, it can be tempting to think we know exactly what their problem is and what they ought to do about it. But the realisation that we cannot presume to judge what the soulful purpose of someone else's experience may be frees that person to discover the next steps for themselves. With the discipline and humbling power of attentive listening, it dawns on us that our own conclusions and solutions are often blocking the much more empowering consultation the person can have with their own inner wisdom.

There is so much we can gather from our times of sadness by listening deeply to ourselves, to others, and to the deep silence beyond. Listening reminds us that rather than jumping to solutions too quickly, it is fruitful to allow time for our own inner dialogue to take place. And we can expand our understanding of what 'dialogue' means to include a wordless and slow-paced communing with silence. When we are ready, we may want to write about an issue of sadness, as a way of having that dialogue and seeking clarity about it. To begin with it will be important to just describe our situation and our feelings rather than try to find solutions or seek advice. At some point we may want to have a dialogue with a trusted person, making sure they understand that their role is to ask you questions about your experience and then listen as you find your own thoughts and words. It will be very important that this person has the capacity to hold their tongue as well as the soulfulness of the space between you so that you can find your own answers in your own time.

Listening takes place in many ways. Watching, noticing, observing, witnessing, daydreaming, staring into space, looking at the night sky, a sunset, a seashell—these can all be forms of deep listening. So too is being awake to symbols, messages and synchronous events. Listening can become an act of deliberate 'stalking', where we ask for guidance and are watchful of outer circumstances for signs and prompts. As you will no doubt have experienced, messages don't always arrive in the letterbox—they can come in all kinds of surprising and even bizarre ways. They may take the form of something you overhear, a cloud shape, a numberplate, a sign on a building, a song, a book that comes your way, an object you lose or find, something that breaks in front of you, a gesture or a smile. Of course, we must bring a healthy dose of common sense to this. While it is not helpful to see signs on every rock, and messages in every numberplate, there are countless ways in which we can hear our own wisdom through outer prompting, if we have the openness to receive the message. Sometimes the messages that come to us when we are listening in this way meet our deepest need and may even save our lives. Nearly everyone you meet can tell a story about receiving an unexpected sign, and while these experiences may be beyond our rational mind, in times of sadness it is especially comforting to tap into the mystery of connectedness in this way.

BREAKING POINT—IRENIE

For quite some time I had been struggling in my marriage. I had been asking questions like, 'What do I need to learn here?', 'How do I need to respond to this?', and so on. The messages I had been getting through contemplation, meditation, books and everyday signs had been about surrender, serving, paying attention, compassion and the like. Painful as these times were, I listened to these 'suggestions' and worked with them as best I could, and they certainly gave me strength and guidance along the way.

Then, suddenly, there was another critical point and the situation was in crisis again. With even greater inner intensity I began asking the question, 'What do I need to do?' I held this question inside myself with a deep yearning and profound need to know. In a 24-hour period I received several not-to-be-missed, loud-and-clear signs.

The first time I asked the question within myself, I was feeding my 11-month-old baby in her highchair. She immediately grabbed a snow-scene toy sitting on the tray and, with a force I wouldn't have thought her capable of, she threw it to the floor. It smashed spectacularly, sending water, 'snow' and bits of coloured plastic everywhere. The last time, I was standing next to my car and a major branch of a large tree cracked, tore and crashed to the ground only a few metres away from me. It was after the branch fell that I really got the message and the signs stopped.

I knew it was time to go; the marriage was over.

As this story shows so dramatically, listening can take on the flavour of dowsing, divining, scrying—opening up the faculties we humans use daily in all kinds of ways we may not even be aware of. Of course, for this, we listen and perceive with so much more than our ears. It is as if we use an internal radar, a subtle inner filament that can feel the atmosphere like the tiny hairs on a fish's head can feel changes in the currents of the ocean. We sense the subtle quality of the environment a bit like a sailor does when he licks a finger and places it up in the air to feel the direction of the breeze. We use our inner radar when we feel something is right or wrong, when we are trying to gauge if a person is motivated by good intentions or not, and when we are able to pick up a hidden agenda or 'know' that someone is lying. As we practise doing this, we become more skilful at it; we calibrate our inner meter to finer and finer degrees.

Similarly, humans are always tuning into the subtle atmosphere of places in the landscape and rooms in buildings to some degree. Walking into a room you can sense that there has been an argument even if everyone is behaving as if there has not. Of course, we are tuning into the subtle cues of body language coming from the people; however, throughout the ages geomancers have spoken of 'place memory', where a location takes on the quality of events that have occurred there long after the people have gone. This can be experienced in sacred places and in places that are inexplicably repelling even though they may be physically attractive.

Sometimes listening deepens to such a degree that you feel you are receiving the meaning beyond the words themselves. Have you ever felt you could understand what was being said even though the person was speaking in an unfamiliar language? It can be like this listening to a highly accomplished meditation teacher speaking in a foreign language, or even a song or poem of great love and longing sung in another language. You can listen to instrumental music in this way as well. As one instrument 'says something' and another instrument 'replies', you can let your imagination run free and create the conversation. Of course, the original composer gives the music intention and flavour by the musical choices made in the score, but *you* orchestrate the words and ultimate meaning of the conversation. The conversation that unfolds in your heart and mind as the music plays may be so effortless that you feel you are eavesdropping on it, rather than composing it.

I have allowed such 'conversations' to lead me out of sadness and into joy by letting the conversation speak of things that set my soul on fire. In this mysterious way, we can invite a very deep and uplifted part of ourselves to guide what it is that we will hear. This strikes me as a subtle yet highly significant aspect of active listening, and sheds profound light on the oft-quoted and easily misunderstood maxim that we create our own reality. (We will return to this theme in the sixth phase of the cycle— 'Befriending Yourself'—when we explore how we contribute to our own reality by deciding what meaning we will give an experience.)

I once read about a musician who said that when he returns home after being away for too long his house gives him the cold shoulder. It knows he has been seeing other houses. He puts the kettle on and it suddenly shorts out; he switches on a light and the bulb blows. This happens when you are away from your own inner silence for too long as well. If you do not set aside times for quiet listening, you may feel that you are about to blow a fuse. You may turn into a dragon-person and find yourself firing up over very little. This is because your own musings have no quiet and fertile place to land and germinate. It is also because silence is a healing balm and we need its soothing presence. But without regular practise it can be difficult to hear what is being offered from within. Then, the resounding silence can easily feel like a block, and rather than listening into a deep and rich quietude, you may feel you are getting the silent treatment, the cold shoulder.

It takes a particular kind of inner posture to be able to hear the silence speak. Just as an athlete or dancer trains their muscles so that their bodies can easefully move through the postures associated with their sport, so too we become skilled at sensing silence by practising the inner posture needed for deep listening. For this reason many people decide to take up a practice that is designed to enhance their capacity to listen. Meditation is a time-honoured way of training the listening muscles. However, when people first take up a practice like this it is often not silence that they hear but an annoying internal commentator giving a running narrative as if reporting on a space mission, relaying a blow-by-blow account to ground control. This internal commentary is often filled with snippets of past conversations, critiques, old feelings of hurt or triumph, clothes to wear, people to correct, projects to complete, and rehearsed conversations to have and . . . you name it, the list is endless! However, we can learn the knack of listening—not to the commentary, but to the silence beyond it.

This requires a gentle but sustained effort to create the space for silence to be heard. It is actually a matter of deciding what you are going to value. You form an inner intention about where you want to place your attention and you practise placing it there. Time and again.

The more you reflect on silence, practise noticing silence, meditate on silence, invoke silence, value silence, remind yourself that this is what you are stalking, the more it will be coaxed into the foreground of your attention.

As you strengthen your intention and capacity to listen to the silence beyond the chatter of the mind—it may be through meditation, martial arts, flower arranging, dance, walking, staring at the ocean—eventually the jangling voice of the inner narrator fades and the whole experience becomes more fluid and spacious. You will have more and more times

SENSING SILENCE

What sounds put you in touch with silence?
What places put you in touch with silence?
What fragrances put you in touch with silence?
What sensations put you in touch with silence?

Take a piece of paper or your journal and write or draw responses to these questions. Now, using your responses to give you ideas, take a few days to collect small items that represent each of these four things—sounds, places, fragrances and sensations—that put you in touch with silence. They may be objects, pictures, pieces of fabric, a postcard from a café, a small bottle of oil, a seedpod, a flower, a quote you write on a piece of paper. Be on the lookout for these items crossing your path or catching your attention. They may be 'found' items that fall in front of you, such as a feather, leaf or stone. You may want to include pictures of the sea, a cave, the rain, a gong, a wooden church, a field of lavender, or a path winding through a forest. Or perhaps a swatch of velvet or silk, or a bottle of rose oil. You may want to include a small bowl of water. These items represent aspects of silence. Arrange them with care on a shelf or on your desk. For the next few days select one of these items and carry it with you throughout the day. It may be a different item each day or the same one. From time to time throughout the day slip your hand into your pocket or bag and hold it or touch it. This item is a private reminder of silence for you. Let the item bring to mind an aspect of silence. Shhhh, don't tell anyone.

when the attending or listening itself blossoms like a flower opening up and filling your inner awareness. Instead of there being a separate and annoying commentator playing to an invisible audience, you *are* the Listener, you are the one who is attending, the one who is aware. You are the Awareness itself. In this way deep listening can be experienced as a state of being as well as a practice.

In the state of deep listening, words fall away, just as a prayer may begin with a question only to end in a state of silence where the words of the question or prayer have disappeared. In the state of stillness that arises out of deep listening one's whole being can become the wordless prayer, the wordless question. Similarly, in the third phase of the cycle of soulful sadness, 'Attending to Stillness—Deep Listening', there may not be a formed question at all. You may not know what it is you are needing to hear or listen for. Later in the cycle you may find yourself inquiring more actively, but here you are continuing to gather quietude, allowing the sadness to loosen the ego's grip on how things ought to be and what you think you want. Imagine if all the crazy unbaked things you ask for were granted; what a mess that would be! Knowing what to ask for is a very valuable thing. For this you must regularly visit a quiet sanctuary within where you can pause and listen—to yourself, to the circumstances, to the silence beyond those things.

To develop the capacity for deep listening each of us needs to find a way of receiving silence, a warm and open place within, where silence can be gathered and contained. We need to find a place inside where the stillness and silence can softly land and nestle. Our ultimate aim might be for our whole being to be that container, but we can begin by creating a simple place of sanctuary within. This stalking of silent sanctuary is a slow-food practice, ripened and simmered over a long, luxurious time, with many delightful companions sampling from the same table. The

> **CREATING SANCTUARY, CONTAINING SILENCE**
> This exercise has two parts. Firstly, you will establish a container for silence in your body. Secondly, you will decide on a time and place to practise silence for five minutes each day for a week.
>
> Let's begin. Sit quietly and think of a place in your body that can be your 'container' for silence. Identify a specific part or area of the body such as a place in your heart, head, tummy, lower abdomen, behind your eyes, in your feet, in your mouth. Or you may think of a gesture that can

serve as your receptacle, such as your cupped hands, or the action of cradling something in your arms, or standing with your arms outstretched. See or feel this place or gesture. Give this place or gesture your full attention for a moment or two. Have the thought or intention: 'This is where I will gather silence; this will be my container for silence.' Feel, see or sense how it will contain and hold silence.

Your task now is to put aside five minutes every day for a week to just sit quietly and let this container fill with silence. Decide on a time of day and a place where you can be still and uninterrupted. It may be in bed at night, or just as you wake up in the morning, in the garden or park at lunchtime, on the train, while breastfeeding your baby. Once you have decided on your time and place, set aside five minutes to sit there quietly each day. Do not do anything else such as read, talk, knit, watch TV or listen to music. Simply bring your attention to the container of silence within you (the place of your body or the gesture you identified earlier). Imagine the silence pouring in. What is that like? How does it feel? Let this suffuse your whole being.

As you stand to resume your activities, notice how your container of silence has gathered fullness. Let your attention return to this awareness of silence from time to time as you go about your day.

most delightful companion of them all turns out to be you—so, settle in and enjoy the lifelong practice of creating sanctuary within yourself.

The importance of cultivating silence as a way of navigating our way towards the deep and lasting happiness that lies beneath the comings and goings of sad feelings is not new. Written over 1500 years ago, *The Rule of St Benedict* is an example of how time-honoured practices can be used by anyone today to find moments of peace and sanctuary. One of the key practices for cultivating silence and deep listening outlined in this tradition is *lectio divina* or meditative reading. As Abbott Christopher Jamison outlines in his book *Finding Sanctuary*, this is the practice of reading a sacred text in a careful and slow way that allows what is being read to penetrate deeply within. Benedict speaks of 'listening with the ear of your heart'. This does not mean giving up the intellect and going with a sentimental or superficial impulse. Rather, as you read you are listening for the true meaning of the words to unfold within your consciousness. You are contained and present, letting the words speak to you of what you need to know for your life right now. This kind of reading includes pausing to reflect and is done with an attitude of receiving the text as a gift rather than as a problem or puzzle to be solved. Benedict recommends holding your questions in abeyance and letting the text question you.

Similarly, journaling could be thought of as meditative writing—you take up the pen as a way of discovering or listening to what wants to emerge. A quiet conversation can also have this quality, when each person speaks carefully but only as insight arises. In this way, reading, writing and speaking can all be experienced as forms of deep listening. For these activities to have this deeply attentive quality, though, we need to find times outside of busy-ness when we can surrender our flurry of thoughts to the discipline of the setting. As you know, it is difficult to listen well in a hurry or when we are not centred and contained.

Can we let our soulful listening stand independently of any answer? People often say in frustration and despair, 'I got no answer, I didn't get any response.' They get hung up on whether any Being exists to hear or not. While you sit in your place of sanctuary—listening, listening—you may not hear anything, or get 'an answer'. Surprisingly, a response or an answer is not necessarily the sweetest 'fruit' of listening. This is a radical possibility, don't you think?

Listening creates energy, generates heat and movement even as it may also generate peace and repose, because it is attention. Our pure non-judgemental attention enlivens whatever it falls upon. It brings heightened awareness. The posture or attitude is one of surrender to the listening rather than paying the dues of listening and then feeling entitled to an answer. With this understanding, it seems that the alchemy, the transformative force lies in the state of listening itself. In this radical approach to listening it doesn't really matter who does the talking or answering but rather that *you* do the listening.

For deep listening to take place, you settle right here in the centre of the continuous flow of time—in this moment, this moment and this moment—in one uninterrupted experience of the present. As you become more fully present, the moment opens up; it seems to become fuller and fuller of itself and some say that it is alive with a benevolent presence, a huge 'Is-ness'. What begins as settling into the present moment and quietly listening there, deepens even further and becomes *attending* to the present moment. Every part of your being is awake and enjoining right here.

Why would we want to pursue the practice of listening and attending so deeply? You will have your own way of answering that. For me it is satisfying, healing, balancing and noble. And I repeatedly forget that until a tiny waft of sadness reminds me! Temporary amnesia takes place as I get caught up in something or other. But when the current fizz of the moment dies down, and especially when sadness arises, I invariably find myself reminded that this is the effort I am to make: to be present and to listen. If I wish to experience the fruit of a quiet mind and an open heart I must make the effort to exercise the muscles involved in deep listening—the muscles of arriving, containing, offering and opening up into the present moment. Listening to others, to yourself and into the Immensity. Here in the cycle of soulful sadness we practise all these forms of listening with the intention of creating the space in which wisdom and insight may arise.

We can cultivate deep listening very naturally during a cycle of soulful melancholy. For a time, our sadness and our acceptance of not knowing loosens the pull of the inner commentary. We become less inclined to be seduced by the problems, judgements, stories and even solutions our mind tosses up, and we become more inclined to listen into the stillness beyond them. One of the precious gifts of soulful sadness is that we can become quiet enough inside to be receptive. In this state the mind softens and clarifies, the nerves relax, the jaw releases, the striving and posturing drop away, craving releases its grip, and the heart opens. The practice of deep listening is mighty preparation for a turning point, an encounter with grace—the next phase in the cycle of soulful sadness.

CHAPTER 7

ENCOUNTERING GRACE—THE TURNING POINT

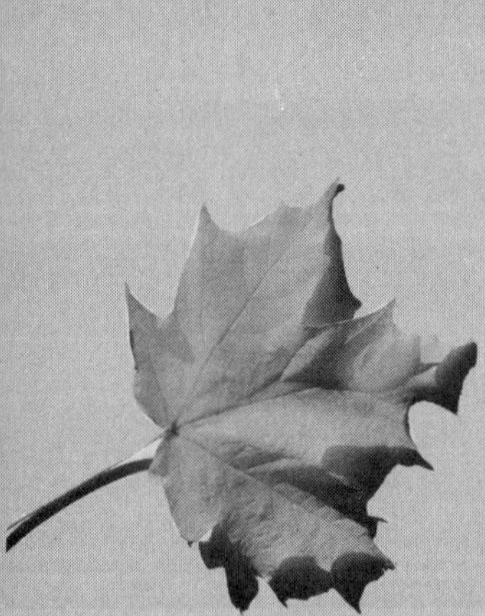

CHAPTER SEVEN

When you take time to pause, gather yourself and listen, something always happens. After a while (it may be minutes, hours, days, or even weeks) *something*—even if it is the tiniest thing—will catch your attention; it will stand out and show itself to you and, amazingly, you will begin to receive the guidance you need.

There is always a doorway of grace. It may take the form of an unexpected sight, such as a bright red balloon floating silently away in the blue sky. You are captivated by it; it touches something inside you. Perhaps you are simply delighted by the contrast of colours. Perhaps the balloon's defiance of gravity releases a lightness of being in you, and a tiny lift of your spirit occurs in that moment. Or it may be quite another moment that flicks a switch inside, such as a genuine smile on someone's face, a dog wagging its entire backside in welcome, a comment someone makes. Somehow, even if it is for a small instant, the moment captures you and pierces the sadness you are experiencing. Mysteriously, when the moment passes it leaves you feeling more open to possibilities, even if you don't notice this shift until later and it seems completely unrelated. A moment such as this is an encounter with grace and it is a turning point in the cycle of soulful sadness.

Of course, we are courting grace in every phase of the cycle and it can happen at any time. The grace in the fourth phase of the cycle refers to a turning point where things shift because of an encounter with upliftment. I believe that such an encounter always follows a period of deep listening and attending to silence, and that's why 'Encountering Grace—The Turning Point' is placed here.

If we are able to stay with our soulful sadness—feel the

longing within it, listen to it, give it our patient and gentle attention—eventually it yields before us; it rolls onto its back and reveals its soft downy underbelly. If we can bear to give it further attention it becomes energising and purposeful. Often the turning point in this transmutation of sadness can be traced to a pivotal moment of grace. In this context, 'grace' does not refer to something we say before a meal, but rather to a catalytic moment—grand or tiny—of insight, release, connection, love or even shock. During these moments it is as if a life-affirming substance made of light sparks inside and nothing is quite the same afterwards. There is a shift within, a movement that calls a halt to the descent that our soulful melancholy has taken us on. The cycle pivots around this turning point and from here we lift off towards the second half of the cycle. From this moment we subtly begin to surface towards engagement with the world of hopeful possibilities once again.

LATTE WITH THE LOT—MICHAEL

The other day I walked into a café to buy a latte. As I waited for it to be made I picked up a magazine and began reading an article about volunteers. The article profiled several ordinary people who regularly volunteer in their community. They were not trying to win awards or gain recognition, but simply wanted to help out.

I had only scanned a few lines of the article when my heart softened and a wave of tingling energy swept up my spine. I was surprised; I had never been consciously moved by volunteers before. As I noticed this wave I reminded myself, 'Ahh, here it is—grace; now really *feel* it, really savour it.'

My heart expanded, my breathing became deeper and slower, my chest opened, my face softened. I left the café holding my latte, appreciating the extraordinary things that ordinary people do. It was a simple everyday moment, but walking out, I felt lighthearted and connected in a way I didn't when I walked in.

An encounter with grace changes the way you feel inside. If you take hold of the moment, whether you experience it as a tiny stir at the beginning of a wave, a blast of understanding or in myriad other ways—it changes you. The fact is, grace is not confined to churches, mosques and religions or even to people who believe in God. It is available to everyone and we begin to experience it more and more as we become skilled 'grace-catchers'. The key is to notice and really savour these moments as they arise spontaneously during the day. This requires a special kind of alertness; a mind and heart that are ready and willing to lean towards upliftment.

SAVOURING THE MUSHROOMS—STEVE

The times that lift my spirit and I encounter grace are either connected with observing something in nature, listening to or making music, or connecting with a lover. Here is an example.

I live in a dry climate; some call it a Mediterranean climate. For me it is defined by how crunchy and dry everything is in the bush. The leaves on the ground crackle under my feet and there are numerous small dead trees standing scattered through the landscape. Last autumn we had an unusual amount of rain spread over a month or so, and for the first time in many years there was wetness and softness in the landscape. I went for a walk in the rain and it was amazing to feel the damp underfoot, to feel the wet earth yield to my step. Everywhere I went I encountered colonies of mushrooms. How amazing are these feisty fungi? So soft and fleshy yet able to displace inches of hard earth to push their way up for their time in the sun. Who knows how long their spores wait under the dry crusty soil until the right conditions came to them? And there they were, all over the hillsides and under trees, whole communities of mushrooms—so delicate and vulnerable, yet so strong. I was touched and walked amongst them in a kind of reverie . . . *and* they were delicious!

In this story the mushrooms were 'savoured' both literally (pan-fried in butter, no doubt!) as well figuratively (delighting in their enchanting qualities of endurance, delicacy and strength). Over and over again it is some aspect of nature in all its beauty and power that can trigger an experience of grace for people. However, it doesn't always happen every time we venture out into the landscape. While we may take the time to watch a beautiful scene in nature—say a sunset—we may walk away completely untouched. This may not bother us at all because we know that this is the way it is sometimes. At other times it may leave us feeling sad and isolated because we recognise that it is a sign of a more fundamental and painful disconnection at the heart of our life. If this is the case, noticing that we are untouched is of great value (some might say that this too is grace) because it puts us in touch with our *longing* for connection. And as many people have discovered, longing is of immense value to the soul because it prepares the ground for an encounter with grace to occur.

Moments of grace often happen out of the blue and are filled with delightful serendipity. We may reach the top of a hill to behold a host of golden daffodils laid out before us, or a field of feisty fungi. Perhaps it is the element of surprise, the shock of the colours, the perfection and tenderness of the scene—but when the experience gets under our skin and pierces us in some way, it has the power to shift us internally. While we can never force these experiences to happen, what we value and what we choose to notice make it more likely that we will be able to catch these occasions when they present themselves. By offering our careful attention to what is before us we are more likely to receive what the moment has to offer. In this way, an encounter with grace can be thought of as a moment of exchange, when something is offered and something is received, and in the process a flash of transformation takes place.

> **MY HEART SOARS WHEN . . .**
>
> While moments of grace often seem to come by accident, what can you do to become more accident-prone? In this exercise take some time to think about what situations and circumstances tend to be fertile ground for you. For example, perhaps you are inspired by athletes putting forth effort at the limits of their strength, people with disabilities getting out there and joining in, children trying hard to do something they have never done before, people speaking up for social justice.
>
> Make a list of things, situations or events that uplift you. If you wish, you can take the help of sentence starters such as:
>
> 'My spirits lift when . . . '
> 'I am inspired by . . . '
> 'I am encouraged by . . . '
> 'My heart soars when . . . '
>
> These occasions are fertile territory for grace moments and you may want to deliberately seek them out or simply become more aware of them as they spontaneously occur in daily life.

A GRANDMOTHER'S MOMENTS OF LOVE—CLAIRE

My heart soars when I hear the children running to the front door calling, 'Grandma, Grandma!' I know love and joy is in the world.

My heart soars when I hear my sons talk as wise, beautiful, responsible men. I know we can all change and grow into greatness.

My heart soars when a parrot suddenly screeches from the treetop, as if to say, 'Hello, beautiful darling.' I know the world is full of surprises.

These are moments of expansion, faith and wonder. These are moments of love.

As adventurers in the territory of soulful sadness, not only are we *seekers*, but it is crucial to acknowledge that we are also *finders*. In the third phase of the cycle we invited ourselves to notice silence and practise deep listening. This is 'seeking'. The pivotal experience of grace we encounter in the fourth phase is 'finding'. We enhance an experience of grace if we are awake enough to really take hold of the moment when it is presented. We catch it as it sparks in our body and mind, and we let it influence how we feel and what we do. We invite it to uplift us and transform our state of being.

The Chinese have a saying: 'Chi follows Li' or 'Energy follows Intention'. This means that if you have the intention to notice moments of grace, this is where the energy will flow, and you will begin to notice them. It is tempting to think of 'noticing' as a passive thing, something we have no control over—either we notice something or we don't. However, in setting our intention to get to know grace, to consider its qualities, to mull over what it feels like and how it arises, we are 'stalking' grace; we are preparing the ground to recognise moments of grace as they arise in our everyday lives.

Sometimes we hear people say that there is so much grace in their lives, and when we look into their faces, even if those faces are wrinkled and careworn, we see that this *is* what they are experiencing. There is a light of softness and fullness that testifies on their behalf. In our noble moments we may be genuinely delighted for them, or we may be a bit miffed or even secretly outraged that their lives are presenting them with access to something that seems barred from our own. However, spiritual traditions speak of the boundless nature of grace, saying that it is ever-present and continuous.

I believe that the person who experiences an abundance of grace in their life has cultivated the capacity to notice these moments as they arise. They have become awake to the skill of catching the moment of grace. It is as if they are 'super-noticers', and they have learnt to reach into the continuous stream of grace and pluck out jewels that can enrich their lives. When we have an experience of grace we are having an interaction with that continuous flow—we have selected a piece of it to be with. And each piece contains the whole. This is why we can learn an infinite amount from one encounter with grace, and why we do not need to have every single possible experience of grace to know it. When

> **PICTURING GRACE**
>
> Using a pile of magazines or postcards, select or draw pictures that represent the 'aha' moment, the 'oh-my-god' moment, the heart-opening moment, the moment of realisation, the turning point. They might be images such as a rocket taking off, a kite, a magic wand, a sunburst, an egg cracking, a heart, a match being struck, a candle being lit, a light bulb glowing, crackers going off, a bud opening, seeds breaking through soil, a whirling top. As you collect or create these images, ponder and savour the nature of grace and let the feeling of it enter your body.

we allow ourselves to have even a tiny encounter with upliftment we tap into the infinite stream of it. So no encounter with grace, no matter how ordinary or brief it may seem, is puny or insignificant.

Because grace is transformative, when people talk or write about it, it's easy to use words and images that seem overblown. It can all seem so high and so far, as if grace is 'other-worldly' and not something that belongs to our everyday experience. But moments of grace can be so simple and unobtrusive; they are seldom accompanied by thunderbolts or crescendos of emotion. Most often they come as tiny little incidents that you can choose to receive as invitations to connect and expand. So our task, especially when we are sad, is not to dismiss a tiny moment of upliftment by thinking it is not the real deal or that it is too inconsequential to stand alongside our sorrow. Rather, we can develop the skill of amplifying the instant of grace by giving it our attention. It might turn out to be the very turning point you have been longing for.

How can we become even more skilful at recognising those tiny moments when they happen? One way is to take the help of our bodies. Our bodies are very good at giving us signals about what is happening, especially when we are distracted by the flurry of contradictory thoughts filtering through the mind. Your body may be the first to let you know when you are hearing, seeing or understanding something that is of significance for you. Is there a surge of energy in your stomach, an intake of breath, a widening of your eyes, a dilation of your pupils, a moistening (or even an ache) in your heart? Does your jaw drop a little? Some people clasp their throat, put their hand to their mouth or their chest, shift in their seat or become rooted to the spot. Some open their palms and look upwards, while others bring their palms together and lower their head, or shrug their shoulders, smile, laugh or waggle their head. What are the body signals or gestures that go with your 'aha' moments?

In the days and years to come, let's continue to notice, savour and describe moments of grace, and ponder the effects they have on us and others. What a worthy occupation of our time!

While there are endless ways that grace can be experienced, I wonder if all these ways share any common features? Do you think every experience of grace might in some way create connectedness—to others, to ourselves or to something beyond both of these—and so help us to shed a little of our sense of isolation and separateness, even for a tiny instant? There are many other words that could be used to describe

---

NOTICING DAILY ENCOUNTERS WITH GRACE

For a few days be on the look-out for encounters with grace. Remember, these moments may be very, very simple: a moment when your spirit lifts, something someone says, something you overhear in a café, something you see, a gesture, a smile, a scene in nature, something very sweet, like a butterfly landing on your arm, or a child saying something. Notice the moment, take hold of it, breathe it in, savour it and notice how it affects your posture, breathing and mood. Notice any sensations in your body. How does it affect your mind? Do understandings come with it? Or perhaps there are no intellectual flashes at all—just a sweep of upliftment, or a softening of the rough edges as if oil is being poured onto a squeaky wheel. How long does the moment remain with you?

Describe the moment and its effects in as much detail as you can in a notebook or journal. As you describe it, you may notice more and more about it. You may want to collect moments of grace like this in a file. You may want to give these anecdotes titles, and occasionally send one as a greeting to a friend on a card or postcard.

this connectedness—we could call it upliftment, communion, oneness, delight, deep relaxation, and love.

If every moment of grace enhances connectedness, what qualities foster connectedness? Perhaps respect and humility are also at play. The following story was offered by a friend and colleague when I invited him to write about a moment of grace.

THE BUTCHER BIRD—JACK

The day we purchased our block of land I was standing beside a tree, having a wee, when a butcher bird landed on a branch directly in front of me. For a moment we made eye contact—the butcher bird tilting its head to one side in the curious way that birds do. It may have lasted 15 seconds but it felt like much longer.

Recently (two years after the first encounter), I was standing in the living room of our partially built house. A butcher bird flew in through the open door and landed on the roof truss directly above me. Again, we made eye contact—gave each other a curious look. As if speaking to an old friend, I asked the bird if he liked our new house; if he was okay with what we were doing. After a minute or so I told him that when he needed to leave he could duck out under the eaves. He promptly jumped across the roof beams and disappeared under the eaves.

My friend told me later that this delightful incident was about seeking permission from a fellow custodian of the land. I believe he was able to experience the grace of connecting with the butcher bird because he had the humility needed to transcend his own personal agenda and put himself in the place of another living creature. The word 'humility' is derived from a Latin word meaning 'soil', so it is not surprising that we can connect with the natural world of soil, birds and animals through the quality of humility. Among many other gifts, our times of sadness help us develop humility and open us to encountering grace in unexpected situations.

In the above story the butcher bird is *encountered* rather than simply seen. 'Encounter' is such a lovely word and it gives us some clues about what an experience of grace is like. You can hear about grace and you can be on the look-out for it, but it is another thing to encounter it. When you encounter grace, the moment touches you, and you are uplifted and watered in spirit. Because of this, whatever effort may have been made, an encounter with grace often feels tinged with magical generosity . . . and gratitude arises.

FAIRY DUST—MARGARET
What is that mysterious something that renews and refreshes?
At 2 a.m. I toss and turn thinking about a sad situation that seems beyond repair. The long night drags along to a gritty-eyed and miserable dawn. Then at 8.30 as I emerge from the house into the day, suddenly it all seems vaguely workable. What magic ingredient or fairy dust has brought that ray of hope?

Grace can enter a situation not necessarily in the form of a solution or an answer but as a tiny shift inside and suddenly you feel that even this situation is approachable, that you can move on from here.

An encounter with grace may feel like a sprinkle of fairy dust, a release of tension, a razor-sharp insight, a flood of goodwill or compassion. You may experience your heart opening or your mind relaxing. Some people say it is like sinking down into a warm bath. But an encounter with grace is not always pleasant or easy. Sometimes it is like a sword that cuts right to the heart of a matter.

THE UNEXPECTED KEY—JOANNE
I have a friend who recently had a bout of depression. We spent much of last weekend together silently sipping tea and holding hands. Soon afterwards she rang to say she was feeling much better and to tell me about something that had happened—something that I think of as a moment of grace.

She went into her local coffee shop and the guy behind the counter asked her how she was going. 'One step at a time,' she replied. He responded, 'Yes, it's not our time to die.' She felt his honest, basic statement was the answer to her prayers. We commented that we get messages from unexpected sources. She said she had been praying for a way out of the blackness and she felt her prayers had been directed to him and he gave her the key she needed at this time.

In the last chapter we talked about being open to messages as part of deep listening. Grace is the moment when the message enters us and shifts our state. It is when the key turns in the lock and the bolted door swings wide open—or perhaps opens just a chink. Grace is not sentimental or clichéd or even necessarily 'positive'. A seemingly dark thought can illumine a situation, if we allow it to do so.

> **A LETTER FROM 100-YEAR-OLD YOU**
> Imagine you are very old and very wise. You have a razor-sharp mind and a huge heart and you are very lucid. You've lived through it all and here you are to tell the tale.
>
> Think of a current situation that may be causing you sadness. Now, imagine you are your own wise, intelligent 100-year-old self. Write a letter to your present self about the situation from the perspective of your 100-year-old self. Address your present self lovingly and with great compassion and wisdom. How will you begin the letter? *'My Dear Precious One, you may not be able to see this now, but believe me . . . '*

EVEN A DARK WISH CAN BRING LIGHT—DAVID

When I was a teenager I came home one day to my dad's house to find the doors open, a gentle summer breeze blowing through and opera playing on the stereo. I could see Dad out the back in the garden and I suddenly had this strong feeling that my step-mum had left for good. It sounds awful, but things had been terrible in the house up until then, so at that moment everything changed and seemed beautiful. I saw Dad in a different light too, and realised that change was possible and that things could be good again in the house. Actually, it turned out she hadn't left; she was just out shopping! But something had crystallised for me. Somehow by clarifying my feelings (even that dark wish that my step-mum had disappeared) I was able to start rebuilding my relationships with both my parents from that point.

Many artists speak of grace as a flash of creativity that comes out of the blue and then ripens over a period of time. The composer Brahms said that once the first phrase of a song had come to him he could then shut his book and perhaps not even think of it for months. When he did return to it, he would find that it had taken shape and was ready to be worked on. The Spanish painter Joan Miró said that the spark for a painting came to him when he least expected it and in the most unlikely ways. With that initial inspiration Miró would begin the painting and then put it aside, facing the wall . . . but it would continue working away within him. Then one day something would trigger him again and he would return to the canvas with new ideas flooding in.

While the spark of creativity seems to be serendipitous—a flash of brilliance from out of the blue, an accident even—the ground has been prepared. Each of these artists has given their attention to their art; they have paid their allegiance and continuously breathed life into their intention to create. This effort sets up the inner conditions for a seed of grace to flourish.

Many artists speak of the gifts of sadness and sorrow. Oscar Wilde, the Victorian playwright who was stripped of his reputation and family, imprisoned and vilified by society, said at the height of his suffering that he felt Love of some kind was the only possible explanation for the extraordinary amount of suffering that there is in the world. What an incredibly painful and courageous journey to the very depths of himself his sadness must have taken him! Some of you will know from your own experience what it must have cost him to arrive at a place where he could pluck such a white-hot jewel out of the fire with his bare hands.

Sometimes there is so much pain; unimaginable sadness, cruelty and tragedy. Why? Since time immemorial humankind has wrestled with this question. Why that person, why that situation, why that suffering? Sadness is not something you get sorted out and all nicely packaged so it's manageable and neat, and you are safe. And grace isn't a magic bullet transporting you out of your life and into a fantasy land. It isn't a lobotomy. Sadness is something you engage with over and again, perhaps stumbling and fumbling but always, in the end, looking for ways to connect with your heart. To me, the courageous impulse towards that is grace in operation.

GRACE ENTERS THE RELATIONSHIP SHOW—DIANA

I am in a dark place this morning. I feel trapped by my life—by this apartment, by our mortgage, by 'us'. What was it I wanted again? I can't seem to remember. I cannot feel what we were in the beginning and I wonder if marriage is even possible in this era. There are millions of ways we slowly wear each other down . . . down into a cold extinct volcano we each go. Pain, disappointment and sadness.

But here is the amazing thing: if I just stay in that darkness watching, after a while I discover the same stillness, aloneness and peace that exists when things are going really well between us. After a while I can't quite remember what it was I felt so aggrieved about. I wind down and something shifts inside. A light-filled thought breaks through the darkness: 'This is simply the slow burn of two people trying to make a life together. In that fire the dross can be burnt off, and I might have a chance to learn to drop into my heart and relate from there, to there. It's no good blaming him. Who do *I* want to be in this marriage?'

This is the shift I was looking for: the small moment when my thinking changes and I no longer want to petition for circumstances to change, but for *myself* to open. There does seem to be some kind of alchemy taking place, just hanging in there with this marriage. Even though it sometimes seems like a long siege, there is such an abundance of grace when a runner comes crashing through the lines carrying a golden insight like this.

In deeply engaging with our sadness we make it soulful. We are challenged to arrive right here in our everyday moments with the seeming impossibility of our lives and value what is truly there, even if it at first glance it seems inadequate. This is perhaps the most profound doorway that sadness can open. It's quite amazing, but even in the midst of deep despair if you arrive right here . . . right here . . . right here in the present moment, you will see that this tiny second is actually okay; it is quite fine, maybe even perfect. The moment of grace stops us in our tracks and we are no longer thinking about the past or worrying about the future, but are right here in the present.

In such a moment your body can seem weightless and fluid, suspended. It is as if gravity has released you and you can let go of being in charge. Maybe this is why many people love lying in a hammock, floating on water, lolling on a swing or lying in a flotation tank. It is as if we return to the weightlessness of the womb. We must all have a memory of it somewhere within us because we have all been in the womb—perhaps not a conscious memory, but certainly a body memory. If we can awaken some of this delicious body memory of letting go, we might become more practised at letting go into moments of grace when they arise.

The opposite of letting go is holding on or grasping, and this gives us a clue about what gets in the way of experiencing grace. Sometimes grasping can take the form of trying to be noticed or win approval, as if others' attention might somehow fill us up and make us feel more complete. You *must* have noticed this, and you must have noticed something else as well: when the party winds down, in the quiet of the night, or even in the midst of a crowd, how sad and empty this grasping

> **LETTING GO**
>
> This activity can be done alone or with a trusted partner. If you are working with a partner, sit in a chair or lie on the floor and ask your partner to take the weight of your arm, your head or your leg. Then the partner slowly and very gently flexes and moves that part of your body. Be sure that your partner is aware how important it is that you can trust them to make the movements gentle, slow and respectful. Try to let go and not pre-empt or resist the movement in any way. Give over to the movement. Imagine that the movement of this body part is no longer your responsibility. You may find that you are able to release the desire to direct the movement more and more as time goes by. Your role is to trust the other person and allow them complete responsibility for the movement. Experience what it is like to surrender control to a benevolent force.
>
> If you wish to do this exercise alone, sit or lie on something that is gently rocking or moving. It may be a swing, a train, a love seat, a hammock, a boat, or other floating surfaces such as a pool lounge or surfboard. Make sure you are going to be perfectly safe, and then surrender to the movement in the same way described above. Sacrifice your control. Let yourself be effortlessly supported and led by the movement.

eventually makes us feel. Even so, it's really hard to stop doing it, don't you think? We learn to catch ourselves at it over and over again, and like a cop in a B-grade movie we have to say, 'Step away from the grasping. Put that grasping down on the floor, right now, and *step away*.' (Hopefully, we will learn to do it without the guttural voice and the cocked weapon!) Letting go of this kind of grasping may be a lifelong learning project but how worthwhile and how soulful that is! Our times of conscious sadness can be of tremendous help with this because they undo us enough to truly face what we are doing.

In this way grace sometimes comes to us as a mirror. This is when we have a moment of searing recognition, such as when you find fault with someone's behaviour only to find yourself doing the very same thing a short time later! Have you ever experienced this? It can be very sobering and saddening to face facts and see your own faults laid bare. All you can do is shake your head and acknowledge that the critical spotlight eventually shines back where it belongs. In his book *After the Ecstasy, the Laundry*, Jack Kornfield tells a wonderful story about a nun experiencing grace as a mirror. Speaking of the dozen other nuns in her community, she said that she liked all but two of them. One day she was in the kitchen complaining to a friend about these two. The nun's friend said: 'You know, these are really not bad people. What is it that gets to you?' The nun said, 'One is lazy and the other takes too much care of herself.' Her friend replied, 'Well, you ought to be more lazy and take better care of yourself!'

That's the thing about grace; it is utterly reliable and utterly honest. You will see and you will hear the unadulterated truth—and you will *recognise* it when you hear it. While such honesty is true compassion, it may not always be pretty. A belly laugh can help because sometimes, when the dust settles, it really is downright funny. In the end this searing honesty tempered with a dash of humour and compassion for oneself and others deeply pleases the soul, and can help us to move out of a faceless, nameless depression caused by a life filled with pretence.

It is so wonderful that we can become more skilled at catching grace in tiny sparkling moments throughout the day. It is grace that we would even want to do this. Then, we seek to imbibe these experiences through the power of our reflection, and drawing on even more grace, we let them light up our life. While these little turning points are flashing and sparking all the time, some extremely fortunate people experience a massive, scintillating encounter with grace that is *the* Turning Point. This encounter has a huge impact on the trajectory of that person's life. There is life before this encounter; and there is life after it. If the person is wise, they will spend their entire life unfolding and integrating the reverberations of that encounter. The grace I am speaking of here is the grace that sets a person on their spiritual path.

For many people, a sustained and painful period of sadness prepares the ground for such a massive encounter with grace. This sadness is not the sadness of things going wrong or desires not being met. It is not the sadness of disappointment, failure or even bereavement. But all these sadnesses may have contributed greatly to leading the person to an awareness of a deeper, more fundamentally gut-wrenching sadness: the sadness of the soul's deep yearning to know itself; the profound yearning of the mind, body and heart to find their true home. An encounter of this magnitude with grace brings the dryness and bitterness of the soul's despair to an end by transforming it into the capacity for unconditional love. It does not mean you will never feel sad again. Oh, no, no, no—quite the opposite. But you will have soothed what I think of as the most stress-inducing, nerve-shattering sadness there is: that of a soul who has yet to find the direction of True North—the Way Home.

If you have experienced this Turning Point you are extremely fortunate. Value it beyond measure, act on it, and fulfill your soul's yearning to the best of your ability. Fall down, get up; try to love from here.

If you have not experienced this Turning Point and you want to, you are also extremely fortunate. You can trust the deep sadness of your yearning to know yourself, to experience unconditional love, to find meaning that truly satisfies. That soulful sadness will lead you to what you are looking for. Fall down, get up; try to love from here.

Whether it is big or small, funny or serious, grace is never insignificant. There is a feeling of rightness about it: the right time, the right place, the right person, the right circumstances. When it happens we marvel at the perfection of it. But it doesn't always happen according to our timetable. You may feel that you are waiting and waiting for a breakthrough that never seems to arrive. Why is it taking its own sweet time like that, you may want to know? The reality is, we cannot control grace.

Here is a clue, though, that wise people over the centuries have embodied; it's a clue that seems to go to the heart of transforming sadness. Rather than trying to grasp grace for yourself, can you make a radical shift and focus on being the vehicle of grace for someone else?

Paradoxically, the process of 'singing up' upliftment for ourselves is fast-tracked by the good will we have for others. Part of flexing the muscle of receiving grace is practising the generosity of being the moment of grace for someone else. Grace flourishes in generosity.

At a workshop in which we were exploring the cycle of soulful sadness, a person asked: 'Why is "Encountering Grace" shown at the bottom-most point on the cycle?' My reply was that once we have been fortunate enough to experience a moment of grace the direction of the cycle shifts as we are challenged to take our insights up into our lives and out to others through the way we live. It is not about pontificating and telling others how to suck eggs but letting the experience of grace flavour our actions and our being. It is not enough to have a moment of epiphany, insight or understanding and then stop there. It is not enough to put such moments down to a random lucky break and then forget them, or collect them like interesting phenomena or party stories. We can do so much more to harvest their gifts. Such moments of grace put sadness in perspective by reminding us that feeling sad is no reason not to be happy. They lead us into the next phase in the cycle because they help us to grow big enough to embrace our life as it is, including all the opposites that are at play.

> **OFFERING GRACE TO ANOTHER**
>
> Think of someone you know who may be experiencing a time of sadness. What can you do to offer a small gesture of good will? Might it be writing a letter, making a phone call, preparing some food, smiling at someone, saying thank you, making an anonymous donation, acknowledging someone's effort. Decide on something you will do to lighten someone else's load, and do it with no expectations of how your gesture should be received. Simply offer it without seeking any reward or acknowledgement.

CHAPTER 8

EMBRACING CONTRADICTIONS—HOLDING THE OPPOSITES

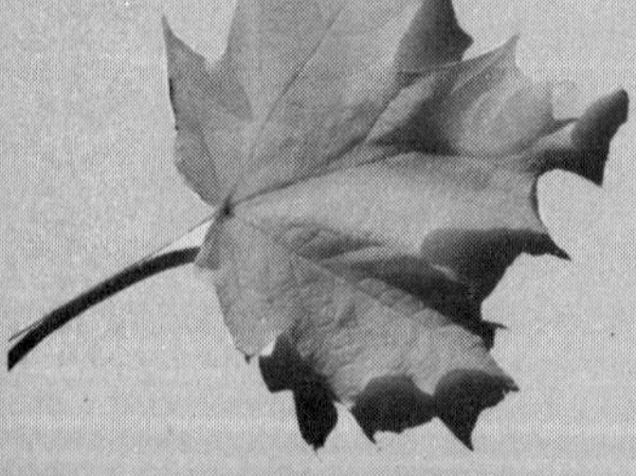

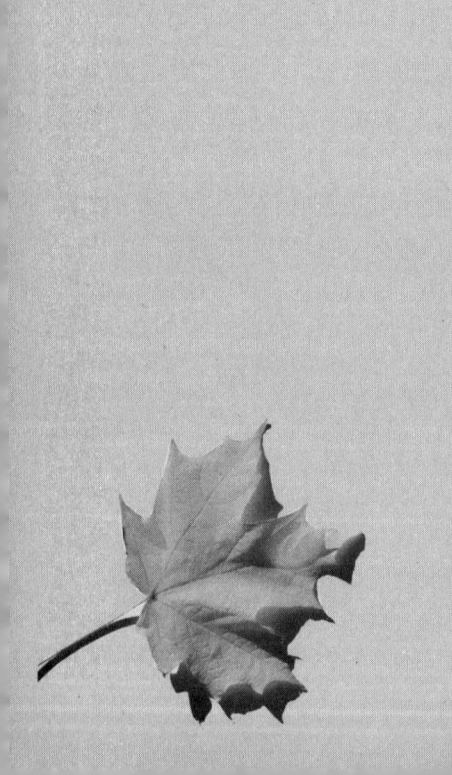

CHAPTER EIGHT

Feeling sad is no reason not to be happy. This may sound like a contradiction but it is a surprising insight that can arise or deepen as we arrive in the fifth phase of the cycle of soulful sadness. How did we get here? Via our longing, the humility of not knowing, the willingness to be still and listen, then, inevitably, a moment of breakthrough or grace. We have explored some of the ways we encounter moments of grace during the soulful sadness cycle. We have noted how potent these moments are, whether they are experienced as a sweet delight, a searing encounter with reality or simply a hint of hopeful possibilities. Grace always brings about an expansion within. It is as if the walls of perception soften and expand. Sometimes people feel this physically as increased spaciousness and ease inside their own skin. Some say their jaw loosens, the tightness around their mouth relaxes, they exhale and settle down more comfortably into themselves.

Because of our own effort to be soulfully present during times of sadness and the brush with grace that inevitably occurs, we grow a little bigger inside. We find ourselves arriving at the fifth phase of the cycle with a more accepting and compassionate way of looking at things. We see that everything has a place at the table and we begin to embrace the contradictions and uncertainties in our life. At this point in the cycle we may feel able to make genuine peace with our sadness, even to welcome it and allow it a legitimate place within our emotional range. We may be more willing to let go of the idea that we should be 'up' all the time. We begin to glimpse that our sad times can serve us as well. We need all flavours because they give meaning to their opposites.

Our journey through sadness to this point has brought a deeper acceptance of pain and difficulty. We can begin to accept that along with joy and success, there is sadness and loss. The more poetically minded among us may see that in some mysterious way beauty and sadness are forever mixed. And to them this perception seems as rich and soulful as a fine piece of smoky late-night jazz. As the fifth phase in the cycle of soulful sadness—'Embracing Contradictions'—unfolds, the rigid boundaries between the opposites soften and blur, and we begin to get a hint that something extraordinary lies beyond them.

GOOD GIRL/BAD GIRL—EM

As a kid growing up I always wanted to be a 'good girl'. When I did things that I thought were good, I was a 'good girl' and when I did things that I thought were bad I was a 'bad girl'. Also, I tended to see everything as *all* good or *all* bad. For example, I decided I was really good at English and really bad at mathematics, when in fact, I was doing well in both. The result of this kind of thinking was that I felt I was a really good person in some ways and a really bad person in others.

At 15 my family and I began to meditate and for the first time I experienced stillness and rushes of peace. I thought, 'Oh, this is really good!' and once again I tried really hard to be good at it so that I could experience more of that good feeling. But of course, when I didn't have what I thought was a 'good' meditation I felt that I was really bad. In this way my attitude towards myself would go up and down with my definition of good and bad emotions and actions. It was very painful and increasingly it dawned on me that this was a real problem for me. At the age of 22 I decided to go to a counsellor and try to do something about it.

Through the conversations I had with the counsellor I began to see that my whole identity was mixed up with my ego. One day she stood up and made the shape of a huge orb with her arms and said, 'You know, your Highest Self contains *all* of these things—the good things, the bad things; the happy things, the sad things. It all has a place in you.' Her words and gesture hit me with such force. From that time on my rigid definitions of right and wrong began to give way and I started to have more compassion for myself.

I began to see that it is a myth that I should be happy all the time, and that if I'm not then something is wrong. My authentic self can be vulnerable *and* strong, happy *and* sad. This image of her arms creating an orb as if holding an enormous ball has stayed with me ever since, and continues to remind me that everything is part of the fabric of life and has something to teach me. Now, instead of thinking 'I shouldn't be feeling this', I watch whatever emotion or thought is arising and try not to judge it. If I am agitated, angry or sad I ask myself, 'What's going on here? What is there for me to see?'

In the late 1970s Albert Rothenberg from Yale University conducted interviews with hundreds of brilliant people including Nobel Prize winners and notable artists. He was interested in what qualities enabled these people to produce such outstandingly creative work. After speaking with all of them he coined the term 'Janusian thinking' to describe what he believed was a key factor. This term comes from the Roman god Janus, who has two heads facing in opposite directions, and Rothenberg used it to describe the ability of highly creative people to reverse the accepted view of things, and to hold two opposing ideas or thoughts at the same time. A highly innovative idea can then be born out of the tension between the two opposites.

There is a wonderful story told by Piero Ferrucci in his book *Inevitable Grace* about the composer Mozart. This story shows how creativity can be released in the play of opposites. Mozart once spent a very enjoyable evening with friends. As the evening was drawing to a close his friends finally persuaded him to write a little music in honour of the happy occasion they had all shared. In a flash of brilliance Mozart produced two canons—one reflecting the joy and sparkle of their evening together, the other representing the sadness of their imminent parting. The friends were surprised to learn that Mozart intended the two canons to be performed simultaneously, expressing the tension between joy and sadness that life so often brings. Mozart was also moved by the heightened atmosphere of the moment; he immediately took his leave and slipped out into the darkness of the evening.

Holding two opposite emotions at the same time does heighten the moment. It's quite a creative act to be able to hold that tension with poise; allowing contradictions, uncertainties and paradoxes to exist easefully within us. It takes most of us quite a lot of practice to master this art.

SEEING DOUBLE? TRY FEELING DOUBLE!—RICK

As a youth worker I know that many teenagers struggle with their emotions. But I've noticed that often it's not *one* feeling that trips them up, but the fact that they can be feeling several things at once. I try to let them know that it's okay to feel several different things at the same time, and sometimes those feelings are going to be complete opposites. We talk about different situations where this might happen, such as feeling excited *and* scared about leaving home. Or about disliking your parents *and* loving them at the same time, about feeling both proud *and* guilty, confident *and* quaking in your boots.

Of course people of all ages struggle with this. Sometimes it's really confusing, especially when the feelings are deep and the stakes are high. One situation where this conflicted experience can be painfully present is when someone close to us leaves or dies. A grieving person may be horrified to realise that they are relieved, even pleased, about the death of their loved one, as well as sad. When it comes to emotions we may wish to be feeling one thing at a time but often it just isn't that way. Human relationships are filled with many layers and it seems that navigating this is part of what it is to grow to emotional maturity—to be able to hold differing feelings at the same time without negating or inflating either of them.

There is a very simple question that most of us are asked, or ask others, countless times a week: 'How are you?' We don't really expect a complete run-down on someone's life when we ask this question. It is more a way of greeting people and opening up the conversation. Most often we come up with a few stock-standard responses: 'Good', 'Not so good', 'Fine', 'Terrific' or 'Terrible'. If you are somewhere in the middle of good or bad you might say 'Okay', 'So, so', 'Not too bad' or 'Can't complain'. However, I've noticed that when I'm asked this question I often feel like replying 'Good/bad' or 'Fabulous/horrible'. It is not that I am a blend of the two, or somewhere in the middle, but I am aware of being completely both *at the same time*. Both are an accurate description of how I am on some level. Now clearly, this could be used to mount a convincing case for my insanity, but whenever I have confessed this to a group of people many of them nod furiously in recognition. On one level they are great and on another they are terrible. So, either we are all a little mad or it's quite normal and sane to experience two opposite states of being simultaneously.

Some of us experience a confusing mixture of 'confident' and 'insecure'. We may carry this pair of opposites with us throughout our lives, and if we haven't learnt to accommodate both aspects, we may try to hide one of them. You'd think we would all try to hide the scared, vulnerable one, but amazingly, many of us are hiding the confident and courageous one. Among the weird and wonderful characters on our inner stage, some will be more acceptable to us than others. Every now and then one of the more unsavoury ones will make an embarrassing entrance and steal the show for a while. In fact, a lot of humour relies on inappropriate characters surfacing at ridiculous and irreverent times. Sometimes we encounter these irreverent aspects of ourselves in dreams (going to school with very strange clothes on), or in sudden fantasies (who hasn't imagined leaping up on the table and dancing like a maniac during a particularly serious and stuffy meeting?).

Or is it just me?

Recognise any of these inner characters?

- Ms Stylish and Cool/Ms Daggy Denim on Denim.
- Mr Fitness/Mr Can't Be Bothered Moving Off the Couch.
- Ms Prim and Proper/Ms Vamp.
- Mr Near Enough/Mr Control Freak.
- Ms Very Happy/Ms Irritated Beyond Belief.
- Ms Vegan Vegetarian/Ms Chug-a-Burger.

It is useful to acknowledge these characters in a good-humoured way because they are likely to throw a tantrum (and throw you off balance) if they don't get to speak their lines in your script now and again. When they feel heard, they are more likely to back off and dissolve into a peaceful silence. So why not enjoy these characters and their outrageous extremes for a short while? They can be a much appreciated antidote to the seriousness of sadness and they may have something valuable to contribute.

Once you have listened to the contribution from both sides of the story you may find that the two extremes soften and come together more harmoniously. The result is a greater sense of ease inside.

> **MEETING YOUR INNER CHARACTERS**
>
> What are some of the outrageous, shy, silly, serious, comfortable, uncomfortable characters on your inner stage? Make a list of a few and have some fun giving them names. Don't be afraid to ham it up. Some of them may not even be human—perhaps a tiger, gargoyle, fairy, toad, sloth, shrinking violet.

> Choose two of your characters that seem like opposites and write a 'character profile' for each of them by listing their favourite foods, clothes, sayings, possessions and activities.
>
> Then, imagine that these two very different characters meet one day and have a conversation. What do they say to each other? What can they learn from each other? How might they coexist more harmoniously? What can *you* learn from each of them? Why do they come and visit you from time to time? It might be surprising and rewarding to hear what they each have to say.

Paradoxically, the more we are afraid of sadness and try to make it go away, the tighter we seem to be holding it and it holding us. But if we are able to relax and accept it, and even bring creativity and humour to the characters that arise during sad times, a shift takes place. When two opposites bump into each other sometimes the result is the 'stunned mullet' syndrome: '*What the*??' The jaw drops, the mind halts in its tracks, the brain blows a fuse, and laughter is the best response. Even in a state of soulful sadness, we *can* let a smile come, and enjoy the play of all the characters who surface to take part in the current story. Time spent visiting with our soulful sadness can help the comic as well as the more shadowy characters within us make their contributions to the story.

Sounds simple, sounds easy. But of course it's not. Janusian thinking—holding two opposite realities or experiences at the same time—can generate much internal heat, especially when there is not yet enough room inside for both of them. But we need this heat. The breakthrough into greater ease eventually comes about because of the friction generated by the two opposites rubbing up against each other. And it sure can be hot in Janus' kitchen!

One pair of opposites that keeps many people on a slow simmer is being aware of the huge rightness and beauty of everything, and simultaneously being aware of a less-than-perfect world with all it ups and downs. It can feel like having one foot in heaven and one on the earth. Can you feel the groin stretch? It's enough to make your eyes water! As human beings we live and breathe the paradox of being very important and also being really quite insignificant at the same time.

Something hurtful that someone says to us can be very significant on a personal level and really completely irrelevant on a grander scale. It depends on whether we pan in on this personal moment or pan out to geological time. Of course, this ability to pan in and out is a very useful skill because it gives us perspective, but until we learn to find the spacious ground between the opposites they will rub up against each other, generating heat and smoke.

There is an Italian word, *sfumato*, which literally means 'going up in smoke'. It is a term that is used in painting to describe the soft, smoky effect created by layers of tiny dots that blend imperceptibly into each other. This technique is closely associated with Leonardo da Vinci's Mona Lisa and her ambiguous smile. Is she happy or sad—or perhaps both? The shadowy *sfumato* around her mouth and eyes makes it difficult to tell. Management consultant Michael Gelb has used this word to describe the experience of holding ambiguity and uncertainty and, in much the same way as 'Janusian thinking', he has identified this as one of the features of an effective and creative thinker. It really can feel like we are going up in smoke as we learn to hold our sadness in an accepting and fearless heart, and it certainly does generate transformative energy. Many people intuitively know there is a precious gift within it, even if they cannot say exactly what that gift is.

The capacity to hold the experience of sadness in a soulful way connects us with others and opens us up even further to the experience of gratitude. It enables our heart to open more and more to ourselves and to others, even if we cannot know the circumstances of their lives or the tragedies they may have undergone. Some souls are drawn to feel the presence of sadness close by. It is as if they are touching on a portion of the sadness of the world. It is *not* that they are necessarily depressive, negative or dour—quite the opposite. They may be deeply joyful people. As they open to love they open as well to sadness and the beauty and impermanence of things—and how sad and lovely that is all at the same time. It is not something to be afraid of or to take a pill for, but it is vital to acknowledge this experience so that people do not have to go through their whole lives fearing that something is drastically wrong with them. Instead they can have a completely different perspective on their experience—a much more uplifted and beautiful one.

An experience of soulful sadness invites us to become more skilful at holding two or more realities with a little less strain and sense of craziness.

THE SPACE BETWEEN

Find a pair of objects or images that seem to you to be opposites, for example:
- a pointy stick and a smooth, round stone;
- a piece of black paper and a piece of white paper;
- a bowl of water and a lit candle;
- a pencil and an eraser;
- a celery stick and a piece of fudge cake;
- a picture of a sad face and a picture of a happy face;
- a picture of a baby and a picture of an old person; or
- a feather and a paperweight.

Choose one pair and reflect on each object in turn for a minute. How does each one look and feel? What qualities do they each have? What words come to mind for each of them?

Then place one on each palm, or place one on either side of you as you sit, stand or lie on your back. Close your eyes if you wish and see if you can be gently aware of both objects or images at the same time. You're not literally looking at them, but rather holding them both in your awareness. You may want to picture them in your mind, or you may simply 'feel' the essence of them both at the same time. Don't strain. It's very simple, soft and natural. It is as if your awareness spreads out and gently brushes or hovers over each at the same time.

After a short while, let the two objects dissolve and imagine you are resting in the middle ground between them. You may notice this space opening up, coming forward and filling more of your inner awareness. Just rest in that middle space for a while.

There can be a tremendous sense of freedom and relief when we are able to sit in the still place between a pair of opposites. But most of us are taken for a rough ride by the opposites many times over before we learn to find that middle ground. One pair of opposites that can give us a pretty rough ride is success and failure. Praise and blame are usually pretty fast out of the blocks as well, followed closely by shame and pride, with boasting and false modesty bringing up the rear. However, a journey though soulful sadness can help us rein in these pairs of opposites by teaching us to let judgement arise and subside without getting hooked into it. Most of us won't change unless things get painful and the discomfort of sadness teaches us to let go and find a path between or beyond the two.

Happy/sad, delighted/appalled, loving/hating, caring deeply/not caring at all. It is a challenge to reconcile the shifting and opposing spaces we inhabit almost daily. But as you courageously practise doing this, sometimes you may feel that a third state is about emerge at any moment—a state that has the potential to lift you beyond either. This transcendent space can be experienced while struggling with the *sfumato* of standing in two seemingly contradictory 'realities'—one sublime and one full of mundane struggle.

THE BRIDGE—JULES

I am part of a regular study group and last week I was telling the group about a dream I had in which I experienced the most wonderful feeling of having a full, open and generous heart. The dream took my breath away and left me feeling exhilarated. As I spoke about this experience in the group, I also talked about how it strongly contrasted with the ordinariness of my everyday life. It made the day-to-day struggle for happiness seem 'pathetic' in some ways, a dead-end road; effort that goes nowhere. The contrast made me very sad because the two feelings were at opposite ends of the spectrum and there seemed to be nothing to bridge them. I talked about this gap and the agony that I felt in the contrast. As I spoke about it tears came because the contrast seemed so unfair and I sensed that I had such a lack of control in returning to the sublime.

However, in being with that sadness, I felt a real intimacy with myself. There was no underlying chatter. There was a booming silence. Then out of that silence I felt tremendous love. I hugged and kissed the people I was with, just because.

I realised that sadness does not have to be a fathomless pit that brings nothing but darkness and despair. It can come and go like lightning and can bring forth great delights. I might venture to say that this learning came about because I was able to feel and articulate both the struggle of putting one foot in front of another, as well as the relief of knowing that the sublime and the divine do exist.

When I left a job I had been in for a number of years, my colleagues gave me a sumptuous, leather-bound, handmade journal that I treasure. They had a quote engraved in gold on the front cover. It is a quote by American author and social activist Muriel Rukyser that we often referred to in our work together: 'The world is made up of stories not atoms.' This quote is powerful because it captures something about the way many of us experience our lives—not only are we the keepers of our many stories but our reality is formed by the meaning we give them. Some of the stories we inhabit complement each other rather nicely, and some contradict each other so much that you'd never believe you are the same character in both movies! Some days you're in the story where everything goes wrong—always has and always will. Some days you're in the story of how well everything is turning out. The trick seems to be in allowing both stories to be present at the same time, without either of them usurping the position of final truth—and watching for something else that transcends them both to emerge.

THE STILL GROUND BETWEEN HIGHS AND LOWS— MARGOT

Following the birth of my first daughter I felt total elation; I was filled with bliss and love. Looking back I see that really, it was 'manic' elation. We were living in my mother's house at the time and for about four months I completely embraced the roles I was fulfilling. I felt, 'I am mother, I am wife and I am daughter', and I wanted to do everything perfectly for them. During this amazing high I slept very little. Then, over a period of about two months I became sadder and sadder as the insomnia deepened. Each day and each night was a battleground for me and I would wake up in the morning thinking, 'I hate my life.' I knew that this was simply not true—I truly appreciated and loved my life and yet I could not stop this battle of negativity. I felt really bad about what I was experiencing—I thought, 'I am a psychologist; I *should* be able to do this!'

Gradually the heaviness and dark sadness I felt wore me down to such an extent that I began to realise I could not climb out on my own; I needed help. I went to the doctor and got some medication to help me sleep. As soon as I admitted that it had truly got beyond me I started to feel better but nevertheless I went to the doctor with a sense of having been defeated.

After about three or four days of sleeping more regularly, the heaviness began to lift and I remember asking myself with a kind of horror, 'Wow, *where* have I been?' Over time I reflected on what had happened and I could see that I really didn't attend to myself during those first four months. During both the absolute highs and the absolute lows I didn't notice and act on what I needed to do to nurture myself. And when I started to go downhill, I tried to bully myself into feeling better.

When my second daughter was born, once again I experienced the high following the birth. But this time it was a deep contentment rather than a euphoric ecstasy. I experienced the beauty of nature in very simple ways, such as the light shining on the leaves of a gum tree. However, once again sadness began to descend as the sleeplessness kicked in. This time, though, I knew the territory a bit more and I began to watch the sad thoughts rather than believe them or feel bad or guilty about them. I was able to allow the sadness to be there; I was not in resistance mode. This made all the difference. I did feel sorrowful but it was sweet rather than bitter or hard. In allowing and not resisting the phase of sadness, I found that I was not so afraid of it—and paradoxically, it did not hang around as long.

I was much more able to nurture myself this time. I knew I simply *had* to respond to my own needs; if I needed to go for a walk or see a friend, then I arranged that. Also, I took hold of inspiring wisdom to help me through. For example, I repeated to myself, 'This too will pass.' This was a comfort to me because it reminded me of the big picture. And then one day I was with a group of friends when one of them said something that helped me see the big picture even more. My friend pointed out that while this sadness following birth is a deeply personal experience it is also an experience that women have had down through the ages. It is captured in the great stories and legends of the 'sorrowing mother' or the *mater dolorosa* as she is known. It was so tremendously helpful to be reminded of these universal figures that give value and credence to my own personal experience of sadness. It connected me with the millions of other mothers and women who have also had their times of sorrow.

I believe that both of these times of sadness following the births of my daughters were experiences of depression. However, because of these experiences I believe I am now better able to balance the opposites of extreme happiness and extreme sadness. I am now more aware of the grey area in between where there is both sadness and happiness, and I bring this to my work with my clients in many ways. When they come despairing about how they have failed or been a bad person I invite them to look again and see how they have hung in there in the face of great difficulty, or been a really caring, extraordinary person in so many ways. I have a greater capacity to *be* with people in their pain and sorrow because of my encounters with the opposite extremes and my own slow movements towards the still ground between them.

'This too will pass.' This practical piece of wisdom comes from a place where neither one of the opposites is fully holding sway. Even if you are filled with sadness, this will pass. Even if you are filled with 'upness', these circumstances too will pass. It is useful to remember that any emotional state or circumstance, whatever it may be, is subject to change. Actually, having a good memory is a key skill when it comes to experiencing the opposites. In our times of sadness it is important to remember that there are also happy times and things to be happy about—even if it seems like a memory and does not have the force of reality right now. As we get to know the cycle of soulful sadness by travelling through it many times, our memory of having been here before, and having moved on through all the stations and back up into engagement with the world once again, helps to dissolve our fear of sadness and build trust.

There is a common perception that happy and sad are a pair of opposites, and at the level of the emotions they are. But there is another level at which a person's sense of happiness and wellbeing is so firmly established that it remains present even as we experience the ups and downs of the emotions. Happiness in this deep sense is not an emotion that comes and goes; it is a continuous note. This is not a way of being that belongs with a rare few people it is far more common than that. Many, many people live with this as their experience and many of them may not have even realised that such a treasure is theirs.

The reason they may not have noticed is that they experience all the emotions such as sadness, regret, anger, outrage and jealousy with the same force as anyone else. They are boosted up and brought down along with good news and bad. They struggle with difficulties and hope for things to work out like anyone else. But this all happens against a background conviction that life is good; they have a deep sense of connectedness and trust as if they have said a fundamental 'yes' to life. It is from this place that it can truly be said, 'Feeling sad is no reason not to be happy.'

This does not make us immune from life's hurts and blows. As you may know with every fibre of your being, an experience of deep sadness can strip us down to absolute bedrock. It can take us beyond our superficial concerns of good and bad, acceptable and unacceptable, to reveal the essence beyond these. Some experiences of sadness are so deep and so excessive that the only response is to meet them with a heart that is equally big and excessive in its capacity to love.

THIS IS HOW MUCH I LOVE YOU, DAD—ANGELA

When my father died the sorrow was, and still is, immense. But one thing I received with that immense sorrow was immense love. I experienced that the source of sorrow is love. When the sadness wells up I don't feel, 'This is bad, make it go away,' but I hear myself saying inside, 'This is how much I love you, Dad.'

This deep sadness took me to the heart of myself. As hard as it was, it was also warm and loving. To me, stillness was at its centre. It took me beyond words, beyond the opposites of good and bad, right and wrong, acceptable or unacceptable. These definitions no longer meant anything to me; they became irrelevant. The sorrow pared me down to the essence of me and that essence was love. Sorrow does not need to be 'solved'. Actually, it is a deep, soulful love.

Through the unimaginable pain of losing her beloved father, Angela somehow came upon a treasure: she unmasked the face of love beneath the face of sorrow without abandoning either of these. What a massive feat! No one in their right mind would ever seek out such a loss, or wish it on their worst enemy, or claim for one second that they had somehow 'got a handle on it'. But some of those who have travelled this road are then able to stand quietly before us in a priceless understanding: that if such a loss arrives at your door, along with it arrives the potential for an equal measure of love. We cannot underestimate the pain and horror of this kind of fire, but we cannot underestimate the love that may be revealed by it either.

When asked how she bares the sadness of her work with the poorest of the poor, Mother Teresa of Calcutta once said, 'I have found the paradox that if I love until it hurts, then there is no hurt, but only more love.' There is a magnificent truth contained in these words. From them we can see that she lived and breathed the transmutation of the opposites. While most of us are not saints by any stretch of the imagination, I believe each of us does have the same opportunity to embrace the contradictions and uncertainties of our lives and learn a little about the soulful art of transmuting pain into love—and our inevitable travels through times of sadness can help us do that.

CHAPTER 9

BEFRIENDING YOURSELF—MAKING CONSCIOUS CHOICES

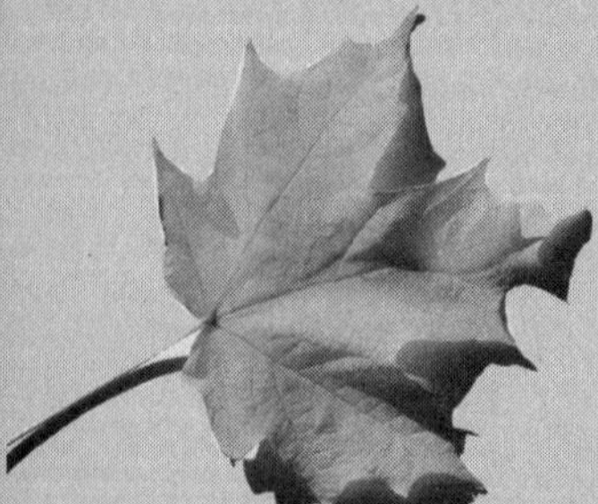

CHAPTER NINE

The gift of acknowledging that many seemingly contradictory things can have a legitimate place at the table is the sweetness of a more tolerant and generous state of mind. We are better able to accept and even welcome our own shadowy characters, and we are less demanding and perfectionist about the way things 'ought' to be. It is a bit like standing before a huge smorgasbord of dishes—while some may make your mouth water, others may not be in the least bit appetising; yet each dish contributes its colour and aroma to the richness of the banquet. As with any sumptuous smorgasbord, though, you cannot eat everything; it's a good idea to choose what suits your taste and what will best nourish you. This is why the sixth phase in the cycle of soulful sadness, 'Befriending Yourself—Making Conscious Choices', is so important.

Here in the penultimate phase of the cycle we are surfacing with gathering momentum from our time of sadness, and even though we are not quite there yet, we are being propelled towards a renewed engagement with daily life. We know that even though there may be a place for everything in this world, not everything is going to serve us well. All things are not equal in their effects so we must make skilful choices. In the light of the experience of sadness that is still so fresh in our mind yet has evolved past its emotional peak, we feel inclined to stand back and take honest stock of our actions and habits. Our attention turns naturally to questions such as, 'What is important and meaningful to me?', 'What do I really value?',

'Which actions of mine are useful and which ones are not?', 'How do I contribute to my own sadness?' and 'What do I want to do differently?'

Such questions require honest reflection, but because we have been softened by the soulful path we have taken through our sadness so far, we want to reflect on them with kindness as well as honesty. I think I have understood the importance of trying to be honest with myself since I was quite young, but it has taken me a very long time to understand the need for kindness to be added to that mix. Emerging out of our time of soulful sadness is an invitation to speak kindly to ourselves and learn how to become our own best friend.

> **BECOMING YOUR OWN BEST FRIEND**
>
> Think of a valued friend. It might be someone who was a friend in your childhood, or someone who is a friend now. It might be a relative or even a beloved pet. If you feel that you have never really had a true friend, then for this exercise you can simply make one up—imagine the kind of true friendship you would like to have.
>
> Now, list three or four positive qualities of the friendship. They could be things like having fun together, caring about each other, accepting each other's faults, supporting each other when you are down, pointing out each other's good points. See if you can think of some concrete examples of these things being demonstrated in your friendship.
>
> Now, here's the twist: ask yourself, 'How can I give more of these very same qualities of friendship to *myself*?' For example, if humour and enjoyment are qualities you value in a friendship, how might you find *yourself* more enjoyable and humorous? What would you be doing more of if you were showing yourself the friendship of accepting your faults, supporting yourself when you are down, speaking kindly to yourself, etc.?
>
> Take one of these qualities of friendship and over the next few days, find ways to give more of this to yourself.

It is natural to think of friendship as something we give to, and receive from, others—and what a precious part of life our friendships are. It is worth pondering, though, that we cannot give what we do not have, and so perhaps our capacity to give friendship to others is in direct proportion to our capacity to befriend ourselves.

TAKING TIME TO PICK TOMATOES—JEN

One of the things I love about my closest friend is that even though she's a very busy person she always has time for me. No matter what time of the day or night I call her, she never hurries me or gives me the feeling I'm taking up her valuable time.

If I was to give more of that same quality of friendship to myself I would need to allow more spaces, rush less, plan less, expect less of myself and others around me. When I take time to do things at just the right pace for the activity, I find I can be present and enjoy what I'm doing. Deeper layers of the experience open up and are profoundly pleasurable, like picking tomatoes for dinner.

Rushing is okay sometimes and it's great to get a lot done in a short time, however I would like this to be a capacity in reserve rather than the default setting. When I'm rushing all the time stress builds up and it takes real attention and effort to wind back to a pace that is spacious and pleasurable and allows me to feel present with what I'm doing.

Thinking about how I might become more of my own best friend I emailed the following question to about thirty people: 'If you were to behave as a great friend to yourself (even more than you may already do) what would you be doing more of?' Many of those people said they really liked the question and sent back a list of key things.

VINKA
- Slow down and become more mindful and present.
- Listen in the silence.
- Count my blessings and be grateful.
- Laugh more and look on the bright side.
- Love and respect myself the way I am.
- Take more time to dream big—knock my socks off and thrill myself!
- Further cultivate the practice of self-acknowledgement.

GAIL
- Affirm myself and delight in my life as it is, foibles and all.
- Have fun making, eating and sharing yummy food.
- Speak with more compassion, gentleness and humour.
- Make sure I have time to simply be.

LEN
- Spend a day (or even half a day) each week that is just creative time and nothing else. Time alone to think, write, potter, explore, create.

SARAH
- Take care of myself more.
- Accept myself more.
- Honour the big and the little things, the public and the private achievements.

VIVIENNE
- Take time out by soaking in the bath and reading something uplifting.
- Take a walk and allow my mind to reflect and to settle quietly into a place of gratitude for the simple things in life such as the family of magpies that hang out on our front lawn and warble in the mornings.
- Write in my journal before I go to bed the things that I am grateful for having experienced that day.
- Laugh and play with my girls.
- Seek out honest, authentic conversations.
- Sing in the shower!

A reliable way to gauge our level of internal friendliness is to listen to how we speak to ourselves. Have you ever done this? It's a very enlightening and sometimes shocking thing to do. Some of us notice that, like 'friendly fire' out on the battlefield, the interior monologue isn't very friendly a lot of the time. Are you habitually berating and finding fault with yourself? It is not surprising that some people freeze into depression under the almost constant barrage of internal criticism. For many people, perhaps even for most people, challenging the harsh internal critic that finds so much of what we do lacking and wrong is an important and soulful thread in learning about our own part in creating sadness.

It is difficult to have a healthy and balanced friendship with someone when either party is operating out of self-loathing, no matter how well covered up it may seem. A visit in the territory of soulful sadness offers opportunities to challenge that sense of unworthiness because it helps dissolve guilt and deepens acceptance and kindness. As we surrender to the journey our sadness is taking us on, some of our sharp judgemental edges are planed off and we can learn to become more of a friend to ourselves and to our life as it is. Being your own best friend is not about being self-serving, self-centred or me-focused. Rather it is about 'self-blessing'. To me, self-blessing means trying to serve the highest in all; it is about the sincere effort to respond in ways that bring about the best for all in a situation, including oneself.

Anyone who has ever tried to create something will recognise themselves in this story of a woman who joined a writers' group, told by Eric Maisel in his book *Deep Writing*. In this group each person took a turn to read their work and receive feedback from the others. Despite trying to soften the critical tone of her comments to the other writers when they read their work, the new group member just couldn't seem to do it. The feedback she gave was perceptive, but essentially unfriendly. Then suddenly she broke through and really heard the tone she was using. There was a soulful moment when she arrived in liminal space and admitted that she didn't really know how to offer feedback that is honest, as well as kind. One of the other writers in the group said, 'It's really hard for all of us; just try to be on our side a little more.' When the next person finished reading their work she responded with a simple 'Thank you.' Those brief words of appreciation were filled with humility and acknowledgement of how vulnerable everyone is when they are offering their best creative effort. In the days and weeks that followed, the woman noticed a change in her relationship with her own writing as well. She still applied her keenly perceptive eye to her work, but she began to feel friendlier towards her own efforts. In this way what she learnt to give others was also what she learnt to give herself. How could this not have a profound impact on her work and on herself in general and therefore to her experience of sadness as well? Such a softening is bound to release a little moisture into every dry internal crevice.

Sometimes people say they feel sad because they have not received the kind of cherishing they most want to receive within a friendship or relationship. This certainly can be a matter for deep sadness and I would not want to diminish it. However, as the story of the writer shows, there is a synergy between what we receive and what we give; sometimes the thing that we think we most need from others is actually the thing we most need to give ourselves.

SWEET SOMETHINGS—CAROL

A few years ago I was chatting with two friends over dinner. We were talking about relationships and, in one way or another, each of us said we felt sad about the relationships we had had with men so far. None of us felt that a man had ever whispered the kind of 'sweet nothings' we were longing to hear. After a few minutes of airing our disappointment about this, we decided that we would try a little experiment. Rather than waiting passively for someone to say these things to us, why not say some of these things to ourselves? So this became our 'homework'.

A few days later I was driving alone in my car and I decided to give it a try. It was surprising how shy I felt about saying these things out loud even though I was by myself. To begin with I couldn't even think of what it was I wanted so badly to hear! I laughed as I experimented with a few lukewarm sweet nothings. Then I started to get into the groove, becoming more and more over the top in my terms of endearment. I really hammed it up; it was hilarious.

Did it replace a lover saying those things to me of his own accord? Hell no! But somehow it flipped me out of feeling 'poor me' and made me feel playful and also full, like I had a tender secret.

What a playful way to befriend yourself and take back the initiative— road rage may never be quite the same! During periods of sadness it is especially useful to deliberately say gentle and affirming things to yourself out loud—and internally—to counteract the nagging voices of negativity that can arise powerfully at these times. This does not mean excusing bad conduct or defending inappropriate or hurtful decisions, but it does mean taking the aggressive tone out of your voice and acknowledging all the ways in which you try your best every single day. Thanking yourself for the effort you make is neither self-centred nor self-indulgent, but an utterly essential ingredient in the dynamics of creating happiness out of sadness. Like noticing moments of grace, cultivating the habit of self-acknowledgement is a skill that is required in order to navigate sad times well. And while we're at it, why not practise saying aloud, and with equally exuberant creativity, the things we appreciate about others as well? Cultivating appreciation in this way brings sweetness and soulfulness to our experience of sadness.

Another way you can discover more about how to befriend yourself in times of sadness is by listening carefully to the advice you give your cherished friends when they are sad. The following story captures the moment a person discovers that the wise and loving advice she wrote to her dear friend was equally for her own dear self.

LETTER TO MY FRIEND, LETTER TO ME—SARAH

I recently sent a letter to a friend who has just been diagnosed with cancer. This is what I wrote: 'My strongest intuition about what you need and what you'll learn, is that now it is time for you to take care of yourself. Fully, selfishly, rightly. You have nurtured your children, grandchildren and husband all your life and I wonder if there has been enough left over to nurture yourself? Now they must make their own way and you need to find the time and the way to put yourself first. Only then can you truly, clearly give to others.

I believe our life unfolds to help us become the very best we can. I know that often circumstances certainly don't look like blessings; they look just the opposite, in fact. And yet with grace, courage and humility the hardest things can change us, teach us and enlighten us. I know this will be the way for you. You are brilliant, beautiful and full of love. There is more than enough for you to give to others AND hold a huge bundle of it for yourself.'

When I looked at what I had written to my friend, I saw that this is also a letter to myself as my own best friend.

Somehow in times of sadness we need to find ways to walk alongside ourselves. Not rushing ourselves forward nor pulling back in recoil either. If, in times of sadness, you don't stand with, beside and in yourself, you may well feel afraid and abandoned. Why wouldn't that happen? Like a caring parent standing right next to a child and not walking away, you are much more likely to feel safe, warm and protected when you stand with yourself and let go right here into the present moment.

There is a big difference between 'letting go' and 'abandoning yourself'. Letting go into the present moment is not self-abandonment, nor is it hopeless resignation. In sad times many people have a habit of wanting to disappear and to be rid of themselves and the present moment. It's a case of, 'If I cannot make the experience go away then perhaps I can disappear.' We have all had those excruciating times when we simply want the ground to swallow us up; to be somewhere else—anywhere else. Picture these embarrassing memories from several people's internal 'home movies':

- You're the bride and you slide over in a great mass of white tulle on the dance floor.
- You leave the bathroom at the airport with a trail of toilet tissue fluttering from under your skirt.
- You lean in for the first kiss and bang teeth with the girl of your dreams.

- Your floating organza sleeve gets caught in his fly.
- You laugh wittily at a business dinner only to spray food onto your potential boss's suit lapels.
- You think someone's thanking you and you start saying 'Don't mention it' when you realise they are thanking someone else.
- You stand up to receive an award and find out that you misheard the name and it's not meant for you after all.

Can the cloak of invisibility please descend now?

These may be lighthearted examples but such moments can cut deep, especially at vulnerable times. Repeated humiliation by others, such as bullying, can certainly give rise to self-loathing and feelings of hopelessness, which, over time, can develop into a cankerous depression. This is way beyond simple sadness and in these circumstances walking alongside ourselves is done by asking others to walk alongside us too. In other words, we need to seek assistance.

It can also be devastating when we humiliate ourselves by doing something we are truly ashamed of. If this happens it is important to feel the regret and acknowledge the deep hurt our actions may have caused, but once again the trick is doing that while not abandoning ourself. The place to start, I think, is to notice the subtle impulse towards self-abandonment, and to respond by inviting yourself to remain by your own side in friendship, even as you honestly acknowledge your responsibility in the situation. Notice, too, how quick we can be to abandon others when they do something we don't like—abandoning yourself and abandoning others tend to go hand in hand.

Sadness can become destructive when it is filled with loathing and we abandon ourselves in disgust, panic and shock. Of course, we are human. We mess up and freak out sometimes, maybe even disturbingly often. See where you may have gone wrong, genuinely apologise and make appropriate reparations if this is called for. But don't sink into self-loathing. Keep standing right there with yourself, with your huge heart, as you sort it through. The cycle of soulful sadness describes a way of being with yourself while finding a healthy and effective way of relating to pain and loss.

A person once asked the fourteenth-century Persian poet, Hafiz, 'What is the sign of someone knowing God?' According to Daniel Ladinsky, in his book, *The Subject Tonight is Love*, Hafiz replied, 'Dear, they have dropped the knife. They have dropped the cruel knife most so often use upon their tender self and others.' What knife? It is the knife inside you that finds you and the circumstances of your life lacking and wrong, the one that wants to cut out a different shape, the one that wants to tighten the screw in your jaw, the one that wants to lob off bits of you and throw them to the dogs. The knife that wants to blame and shame, defend and attack.

My experience so far is that I haven't always been able to stop myself from grasping the knife. Finding fault, especially with myself, is a very strong habit. But while I may not be able to stop myself, I can challenge the truth of the internal comments; I can stop animating them, breathing life into them, investing them with any claim to reality.

This is befriending yourself: knowing that your harsh comments are not the truth about you or your life, knowing that it is especially tempting to buy into them when you are sad but in quite a short time you will see things differently, making choices to speak to yourself honestly yet kindly, taking your own best advice to heart, practising qualities of friendship towards yourself, acknowledging your own sincere efforts, and standing right there with yourself. All these things are part of becoming your own best friend.

In addition, I believe that one of the most potent ways to befriend yourself is to take time to understand how you create meaning. Understanding that each of us is the meaning-maker in our own life puts us in charge and challenges the feeling of powerlessness that accompanies depression. In the presence of pain and sadness, meaning can be our way through, as illustrated by the following story related to a group of students by therapist and teacher David Johnson.

MEANING CAN BE A WAY THROUGH

An elderly man came to counselling suffering from a lingering depression. Some time earlier his wife and beloved companion of many years had died. While the shock of her death and the peak of his grief had passed, this man felt that without his life partner his life simply had no meaning. The counsellor listened quietly to the man speaking about the absence of meaning in his life. Then, in a moment of inspiration the counsellor asked him, 'Tell me, what do you think your wife would be feeling if you had died first?' The elderly man replied, 'Oh, she would be feeling as lost as I am. She would be suffering deeply just as I am suffering. I am sure she would also be feeling that her life no longer had any meaning.'

After a moment of silence the old man simply said, 'Thank you.' It had suddenly dawned on him that because he was enduring her absence, his wife was spared the suffering of losing him. This was enough for him. He did not need to know *why* his life had turned out the way it had; only that his life was now meaningful to him as a service to his wife. He had found a meaning in his experience that could sustain him.

Many people think of meaning as a passive thing—something they have no control over, something that falls out of the sky. And sometimes, oh joy of joys, it does seem to do this! For example, some extremely fortunate people have a massive and life-changing experience of spiritual initiation that creates a seismic shift in the meaning of everything else from that moment on. For others an accident, a death, a birth, or an illness can bring about a profound change in their sense of meaning. Whether we have experienced such profound shifts of meaning or not, I believe meaning is something we are called upon to actively create, day by day, in very simple, yet profound ways. This is because making meaning is connected to wellbeing. Making meaning is also directly related to our values and if we do things over a long period of time that don't support what we truly value, a lingering sadness can arise. This causes a vague feeling of dissonance and people will often say something like, 'I can't put my finger on it but I just feel that there is no meaning in my life.' When we are not making meaning over an extended period of time, depression can sneak up on us. In fact, Eric Maisel suggests in his book *The Van Gogh Blues* that as soon as you feel depression arising, it is useful to recognise this as a meaning crisis.

Because meaning-making is connected to our values, an effective way to embark on a meaning-making quest or respond to a meaning crisis is to reflect on our values, identify what natural and enjoyable actions we can do to serve those values, and then build those actions into our day.

MAKING MEANING

A meaning-making quest often begins to take shape with a question we ask ourselves about our values, so that's the first of three steps in this exercise.

MEANING-MAKING QUESTIONS
Choose *one* of these questions:
- What's most important in my life?
- What really matters to me?
- What do I really care about?

- What means the most to me?
- What are my values?

Once you have chosen a question, write it in the middle of a large sheet of paper. This is your graffiti sheet. Put it on the floor, up on a wall or noticeboard or place it over a table or desk like a tablecloth. If you have it on your desk feel free to put other things on top of it such as your laptop, notebooks, pens, coffee cup, a sandwich. The idea is to randomly scribble on it when something occurs to you about the question. Leave it there for a while (three days? a week?). During that time keep turning the question over in your mind and write, draw or paste onto the sheet any words or images that relate to the question.

MEANING-MAKING VALUES
When you are ready, clear the accumulated objects and crumbs off the graffiti sheet and have a look at it. Are any themes emerging? For example, there may be several words or entries on the sheet that relate to a single topic such as 'Family', 'The Environment', 'Keeping Fit', 'Connecting with Friends', 'Money', 'Fun', 'Social Justice', 'Balance', 'Solitude', 'Animals', etc. See if you can identify about three key topics or 'meaning values'. Keep it simple—just go for a small number of your most important meaning values. Then take some regular-sized blank pieces of paper and write the name of a different value as a heading at the top of each sheet.

MEANING-MAKING ACTIONS
Here's the last really important step: under each heading, list activities you *already do* that support this value. Take a look at the simple, ordinary, perhaps everyday things you do, with fresh and

> generous eyes! They may not be as insignificant as you think. If you wish, you can add a small number of simple, achievable *new* activities, but the focus is on enhancing the value of what you already do.
>
> The actions you have written down are your meaning-making actions. They may not be things you ever thought of as meaning-making actions. For example, if one of your meaning values is 'Connecting with Friends', then having a cup of coffee in a café with a friend is a meaning-making action. Even seemingly mundane activities like taking a walk or a nap can be seen as meaning-making actions if they consciously serve 'Balance' as a cherished value.
>
> Now that you have an idea of what your meaning-making actions are, think about how you might want to cherish them and build more of them into your schedule.

THE LITTLE THINGS ARE THE BIG THINGS—LAUREN

It was a real eye-opener for me to think of some of the very simple things I do in my life as meaning-making activities. I had never thought of them that way and now I see that many of the little things I do are way more important than I thought they were. One of my values is 'Turning Inside'. I was really surprised when I wrote 'swimming' down as a meaning-making activity under this heading. I had never thought of doing laps as 'turning inside' but it really is because when I'm in the water with my ear plugs and goggles on, I'm drawn inside. I see my swims now as more than just a way of keeping fit. Even having a coffee by myself is more meaningful to me now, rather than a reason to feel lonely. It's important not to let the little things slip away because when you think about it in this way, they're not so little.

The crowning glory came for me one day when one of the twins walked in as I was sitting on the couch with my feet up staring into space. He said, 'Hey Mum, you're not doing anything important, can you find my gym gear for me?' I said, 'Well actually, I *am* doing something important—I'm making meaning!'

Being guided by our meaning values is fundamentally health-promoting because these actions tend to reduce internal chaos and dissonance and help us feel authentic and purposeful. People are essentially meaning-seekers and meaning-makers. When we are doing things that reflect our values we are making meaning and befriending ourselves.

It is so tempting to think that someone else's glamorous and 'important' life must be full of meaning, but it is often the small things of ordinary lives rather than the grand sweeping gestures that are actually the most reliable containers of meaning in the end. Sad times can play a role in helping us to drop the heavy bundle of self-importance necessary to see ordinary things in this generous light.

Consciously creating meaning is a powerful thing to do. It invites each one of us to be in the driver's seat of our own life. We may not be able to change what has happened in the past but we can be the keepers of what we decide our experiences will mean for us. We can decide that a sad time does not mean that our life is ruined. We can decide that it is life expressing itself uniquely through us and that there is always something soulful to experience and learn.

Making meaning is not a static thing. It is constantly evolving and shape-shifting and sometimes our meaning values and actions need to be updated, tossed out or added to, especially during a time of transition or big change. An experience of sadness can be the soul's reminder that making meaning is now critical. If we know what actions help us make meaning then we will be in a better position to come to our own aid.

REFRAMING VALUES—ANNE

I met a person who had been a sister in a religious order. After many years of turmoil and soul-searching she finally decided to leave. She went through a very difficult period that involved a complete change in her lifestyle. She said that even though she tossed out many of her accepted beliefs, her core meaning values did not fundamentally change. I asked her what she meant. She said, 'While I was in the order I was governed by the three vows of chastity, poverty and obedience. I had always taken these vows very much to heart and even when I left I did not want to abandon them. But I had to reframe them as values that I felt were appropriate to guide my new life. And so chastity, poverty and obedience became loyalty, simplicity and humility.'

Why is it that even when we know what actions are most beneficial, we don't always choose to do them, even when we really want to? Many, many factors make up the complex mix of human motivation and life is rarely all neat and tidy. While we may know that our meaning-making actions are really important to our wellbeing, they are often the very things we have the greatest difficulty in maintaining, especially when we are sad. On this never-ending meaning-making journey you may feel you take a couple of steps forward and then one back. It's enough to make you feel soulfully sad sometimes! And yet, the sincere and ongoing effort we make to align our lives with our deepest values, and balance our seemingly opposing values, is itself, full of soulful meaning, and therefore deeply enriching.

Times of soulful sadness help us to gather the will to make conscious choices. It is as if the soulful sadness burns off some of the dross of inertia and for a time there is greater clarity and capacity to act. The bottom line is that the pain of sadness prompts us to examine what it is we are doing and try to change.

Here in the second-last phase of the cycle it is about riding the momentum of the sadness you are now emerging from, and using that energy to take hold of your life in a more deliberate way. You focus on how to be your own best friend, make conscious choices and take up your role as the meaning-maker in your life. By engaging with your sadness as it evolves through its phases, your attention and energy will naturally begin to flow back out into the world. As you get ready to apply the understandings you have gained and offer yourself 'out there' once again, you will be drawn even further into the expression of your unique identity through the qualities of your presence and the service you offer in the world.

CHAPTER 10

THE WORLD CALLS—OFFERING

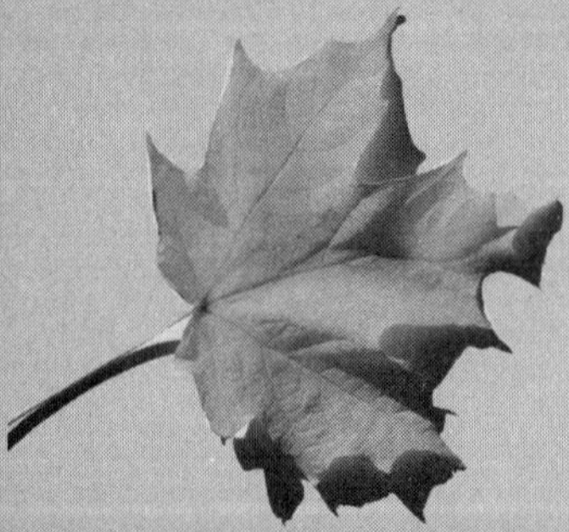

CHAPTER TEN

As we enter the final phase of the cycle we gather up the internal resources to step out into the world with renewed enthusiasm, taking the gifts of soulful sadness with us. Building on the clarity we gained in the previous phase about our values, choices and how to offer friendship to ourselves, we now focus on what we want to offer the world. We have followed the thread of soulful sadness through each of its phases and now we can sense the world calling us to sharpen our intention and purpose. We are about to embark on the seventh phase in the cycle, 'The World Calls — Offering'.

In this last phase of the cycle we look back over the territory of sadness we have travelled through and ponder questions such as 'What did I learn?', 'What might I want to do differently?', 'Who am I now?', 'What do I have to offer the world?' and 'What's the next simple step?' It is a period of consolidation where we have the opportunity to reflect on our goals and life purpose in the light of what we have gathered from our time in the crucible of sadness.

As you may have experienced, there can be considerable overlap between the phases in the cycle. You may have noticed a dramatic difference in flavour between them or you may feel that one slides imperceptibly into the next, with the merest hint of difference. The phases may happen out of order; some may linger for quite some time, while others go by in a flash. So, you may be wondering, 'How do I know when I am entering the last phase of the cycle?'

The following comments reveal some of the signs.

- 'I notice I'm more positive about the thing that was bringing me down. I start thinking, 'Yes, maybe I can try something different there.'
- 'My mood becomes more optimistic, and ideas and plans bubble up.'
- 'I feel lighter, like maybe everything's going better than I thought.'
- 'I want to reach out to people and connect with them again.'
- 'Colours seem brighter and I feel emptier—like it's time for a fresh start.'
- 'I feel like answering my phone and returning messages again!'
- 'I find myself in the kitchen cooking food and thinking about inviting people over for a meal.'
- 'I'm not as tired and I've got some energy and enthusiasm.'
- 'I feel stronger and my workout at the gym gets more energetic.'
- 'I think about what I really want to do with my life and I start getting more concrete about it by writing down my goals.'
- 'I ask myself, 'Okay, what's the first step I'm going to take?''

The end of the cycle is marked by a return of energy and optimism where people look for ways to participate rather than to withdraw. Some people find themselves drawn to large questions of destiny and identity, while others experience a simple impulse to reach out to others or try something different. As the cycle nears its end you may find that you have made, or are about to make, a life-changing decision. Or you may simply find yourself in a place where things seem more workable. Whatever the experience, the cycle of soulful sadness brings you to a point of renewal where you are becoming ready to step out into the world again.

At the first stirrings of enthusiasm and renewal it is tempting to want to put the sadness behind us as soon as possible and move on. There can be a strong impulse to pick up our bundle and march on out into the world, breathing a sigh of relief and declaring, 'I'm baaaack!' When the chaffing begins to fade and we feel that we are off the hook, it's easy to let all the learning fade along with the discomfort. Of course, this is natural because sadness can be painful and we're pleased to see its retreating back. But the pain of sadness is valuable because it forces us to engage with it in some way—would we really change without it?

Of course, it is a good thing to let your sadness transform and flow forward into renewed enthusiasm and action. That's the whole idea! But do not leave the cycle too soon, or rush to share your learning with others before you have consolidated it within yourself. You have paid your dues to sadness with your careful and courageous attention, so don't let the gifts of this time slip through your fingers. Before you pull out of the last phase of the cycle just as it's beginning, take some time to become aware of the terrain you have travelled through, what you have learned there and how you might want to bring that forward into your daily life.

> **MAPPING THE LANDSCAPE OF SADNESS**
>
> Sit quietly in a place where you will be undisturbed for a while. If you wish, make a cup of something warm, gather up your journal or paper and pens, and put on some quiet music. When you're settled, take a few minutes to think back over a time of soulful sadness that has finished or is drawing to a close. You can write if you wish or simply sit and ponder. The following questions will help you reflect back on this time.
>
> - When and how did you first notice the feeling of sadness coming on?
> - How did it change over time?
> - What were the main features or key turning points of this time?
> - Did you notice the sadness moving through the various phases of the cycle?
> - Were any of the phases particularly prominent?
> - What sorts of things did you do during the time of sadness?
> - What was helpful and what was not?
> - If the time of sadness has ended, how did you know it was coming to a close?
>
> **TIMELINE OR MAP**
> Now, draw a horizontal line across the page. This is a timeline for your experience of sadness. Place the key features of the experience along this line in the order they happened. Alternatively, you can draw a map with a road meandering through. This road represents the experience as it unfolds. Mark and name the key features of the landscape in your

> own creative way, such as the 'Cave of Longing', 'Swamp of Liminal Space', 'River of Grace', 'Twin Peaks of the Opposites', etc. Take the time to be imaginative with your naming and drawing. The timeline or the map will help you to capture a picture of this time.

Having travelled through the terrain of sadness we may find we have arrived at a place where very little has outwardly changed, a place where all the street names remain the same—Same Work, Same Home, Same Partner, Same Routine—yet, undoubtedly, everything has been subtly affected by what we have experienced. Or we may have arrived at a place where things have changed or are about to change quite dramatically—a resignation, a relationship split, a new career direction, a change of residence. You may have sensed that these changes were brewing for quite some time, and the period of soulful sadness has served to bring them to a head, or the changes you are embarking on may be utterly unexpected and surprising. Wherever you now find yourself, it is important to take stock of what you have gathered along the way before you head off again.

By the time an experience of soulful sadness is drawing to a close, you may have a sense of what it is you can take away from this time. Often, one or two 'hot' understandings, lessons or insights readily stand out. Equally, you may have no idea at all, or only the beginnings of an intuition about what the whole experience was about. Sometimes it takes a great deal of time, perhaps a whole lifetime, to understand fully what the gifts of an experience of sadness may be. So, in pondering what you might take away from an experience of sadness, do so with gentleness and with the intention of discovering only what is ready to be discovered at this time. You can always come back and uncover more further down the track.

> **HOT TAKEAWAY**
>
> Using the same experience of sadness as the last exercise, see if you can discover what lessons, insights or understandings you can take away from this time. The following questions may help you ponder this.
>
> - What single thing came to my attention most strongly?
> - What was I invited to 'get bigger' about?
> - What did I learn during this time?
> - What will I take away from this experience?
>
> See if you can write down one or two key insights you can take away from this time.

NEVER LET FEAR STOP YOU TAKING THE NEXT STEP—ALEX

My job had not been working out for quite some time and this had been causing me great distress and sadness. It was a job I had loved and valued for many years and I was afraid to let it go. Where would I find another job as good? How would we survive financially? Resigning from that job was one of the most difficult decisions I've ever made. I wondered, 'Do I jump in further or do I jump out?' I thought about it almost constantly. I looked for signs—and received them over and over—yet I would always circle back into the liminal space of not knowing what to do. I kept thinking, 'One day I will know for sure which way to jump,' but that absolute certainty never arrived.

One morning I woke up and said to myself, 'Enough is enough. Today is the day I will resign.' In the end I made this decision not because I was sure it was right—I never had the luxury of being sure—but because I was so sick of going around and around that I simply had to make a move.

It turned out to be a very good decision, and when I think about the key things I took away from that difficult time I would say: 'Never let fear stop you from taking the leap you know you need to make; holding on too long does not serve anyone; and trust that the next step will be there.'

What you choose to extract from an experience is extremely significant. When an experience is taken inside and filtered through your heart, mind, body and personality, it affects the quality of your presence and your actions. It becomes part of the expression of your unique soul and shapes what it's like to live inside you and be around you. When all is fundamentally well in a heart and soul, eventually a natural pull to want to give to others will follow a time of retreat and consolidation. The leading lights amongst us tell us that the human soul blossoms with the fulfilment and joy of making a generous contribution.

People often come to the end of the cycle sensing that there is something they must do; the next step in their life is calling them. There is a nagging pull letting them know they have a job to do, a destiny to fulfil—no matter how humble it may be. A period of sadness is a natural time to pause and re-evaluate priorities and goals. In the last chapter we asked, 'What are my values?'; now we ask 'What is my purpose?', 'What is my unique soul's expression?' and 'What do I now have to offer?'

This is no small thing; it is a powerful thing and, I believe, a sacred thing to offer a bright piece of yourself to the world through an energised point of learning. And when this is offered back to others with a selfless spirit, then it can be called 'service'. Service happens naturally when we take the time to walk in someone else's shoes, and our own experiences of sadness help us develop the empathy needed to do that. It seems to me that one of the great uses of sadness is that it pares us down a bit so that we can, if we choose, discover a little more about how to offer service from the heart and from the uniqueness of who we are.

The last phase of the cycle is an appropriate time to engage with the question of what it is we are here to do, hopefully without self-inflation, yet without self-effacement either. Some people's service brings them fame, even if they have not sought that out in any way, while the offerings of others remain private and unacknowledged. Even if someone's service is invisible to everyone, it has great transformative power for the person offering it and for those receiving it. Everyone around them benefits when a person offers their unique strengths generously into the world in some way. It doesn't matter if a grand destiny awaits or not because everyone gathers respect for themselves and creates a potent antidote to sadness by looking to their strengths and asking, 'What can I offer?'

ONE HUNDRED PER CENT PRESENT—ANTHONY

I was doing a research project in the emergency department of a large hospital. I was very struck by the charge nurse there. There was not one iota of her that was not being a charge nurse. She was one hundred per cent present, boots and all; she held nothing back and yet she was calm and approachable. Everyone responded to her with respect and even the doctors deferred to her. She lifted the performance of the team and the atmosphere of the whole emergency department. It was very inspiring to see the huge impact she had by giving herself completely to her role.

WHAT YOU OFFER

What are your qualities and gifts? Is a sense of purpose calling you? What will you offer? Here are some questions to help you play with possibilities.

AS A CHILD . . .
- When you were a child, what sorts of things did you like doing?
- Did you have a dream about something you wanted to become or do?
- What were you naturally good at?
- Can you remember a moment when your heart soared?

AS AN ADULT . . .
- What strengths, skills and material resources do you have now?
- How might you share these with others?
- What makes your heart sing?
- Is something calling you?
- Is there an important thing in your life that you have not yet done?
- What would you most want your child to receive from you?
- If you could offer one thing from you to the world, what would it be?

Actions that enable you to be the best version of yourself are very powerful. Because they are in accord with your very soul, you feel fully present. You feel authentic, more truly yourself. You have a sense of being in the right place at the right time. This is not only experienced in the workplace; it might be experienced in myriad other ways such as sewing, cooking, woodworking, gardening or caring for children. Whatever the vehicle, a deep happiness comes about when your actions express your unique gifts and purpose.

For actions to truly serve and bear fruit without a sense of burden and layer upon layer of 'stuff', they must be accompanied by a spirit of offering. However, we cannot sustain a spirit of offering without containment and a healthy dose of practicality. It is important to realise that what we may want to offer can far overreach what we are able to sustain emotionally and physically. Certainly our ideals can far outstrip what we can embody. Of course our ideals are vital because they encourage us to be the best we can be. But looking back, I see that it is the incapacity to contain that causes my 'bright' actions to fade, leading me into another cycle of soulful sadness as the longing for balance and connection reasserts itself. Ah, well. The lessons keep on coming.

You may arrive at the end of the cycle not knowing what the lesson is, not knowing anything more about your life's purpose or even where you need to be heading next. You may arrive at the end of the cycle with more questions than answers. If this is the case for you, look among the questions. You may well find a question there that turns out to be much more of a catalyst than any answer could be.

The right question at the right time is a very powerful thing. Such a question creates a kind of interior rendezvous with your own inner wisdom. You know it's the right question when it captures your attention in some way. It might strike you as surprising, intriguing, shocking, exciting, funny, ridiculous or scary, but you keep coming back to it. Some people recognise that a particular question is potent for them by the tiny flutter of excitement they feel in their belly when they first encounter it. Some questions can be thought of as our soul's theme questions because we return to them over and again at different times in our lives—perhaps never finding one convincing answer, but a variety of different responses along the way. Even if no answer ever comes, the right question at the right time can open doorways into unexpected possibilities and ideas, leading us inevitably to the next step.

When the highly creative and eccentric author, Gertrude Stein (1874–1946), was lying on her deathbed, her long-time companion, Alice B. Toklas, said to her, 'Now for the answer.'

Gertrude replied, 'No, now for the question.'

The process of framing a question is a matter of honing and shaping, finding just the right words to express the question mark inside. Then, after a while, there is a sense of completion; the question is as close as you can get to the nub of it, and you just sit with it. You hold it gently. For a question to work well you must really want to know, but not in a petulant 'Tell-me-now!' sort of way. You must offer something to the question—your sincerity, your authenticity. After a while maybe the words of the question disappear altogether but the feeling of the question remains with you, almost as a living presence. Your whole being wants to know, and this seeking, coupled with the effort you put into really nailing the question, helps to create the container for the response to flow into. Then you simply wait.

HOLDING THE QUESTION—NERIDA

When I find myself struggling with something, with emotions ragged and mind racing to blame myself or others, or making things wrong somehow, if I can stop long enough to notice what I'm doing I like to ask myself: *What is this really about?*

When I ask this question it usually takes some time to sink through layers of emotion and reaction to find what feels like a core truth, or several core truths. Sometimes this process may go on over a day or so and burrow deeper as I hold the question while I go about my day.

I believe a sincere call always draws forth a response. To me it doesn't really matter where that response comes from, but more that we put forth the effort to frame the question and then recognise the response when it comes—whether it is a blinding flash of insight, a passing comment made by a child on a bus, or the way a leaf falls. While there is an art to framing a question, an even greater art is contained in being able to recognise a response. For life's big questions such as 'Who am I?' and 'Why am I here?', it's rarely a case of final solutions that enable us to dust off our hands and put an end to the matter; it's more about *connecting* with the mystery rather than *solving* it.

WEIGHTY BURDEN OR EXHILARATING OPPORTUNITY?—PETER

I was driving along in my car listening to an interview on the radio with Peter Hillary, son of Sir Edmund Hillary, the famous New Zealand mountain climber. Peter was speaking about his experience of trekking to the South Pole with a small group of companions. He described the awesome ruggedness of the terrain and the complete failure of his personal will to 'conquer' it. He spoke of the strange soulful peace of that, along with the overwhelming alienation he felt in this landscape he described as a 'ghost world'. He said that in that white expanse of extreme sensory deprivation, relationships between the people in the group broke down to the point where the trekkers could hardly bear to speak to each other. He went on to describe the horror of this and his subsequent mind-bending brush with near insanity, including nightmares and hallucinations.

The interviewer paused at the magnitude of Peter's story, and then asked the following question: 'Looking back on the whole experience now, is it a weighty burden or is it an exhilarating opportunity?' I stopped the car and grabbed for pen and paper to write this fantastic question down. This seemed to me to be THE question for each and every one of life's extreme challenges, even if they do take place behind suburban doors rather than on the ice fields of the Antarctic.

I waited with bated breath for Peter's reply. The answer he gave was worthy of the question. He said, 'It is both.'

Is it a weighty burden or an exhilarating opportunity? A question such as this is a 'living question' because it has the habit of reverberating, maybe for years. I wouldn't mind betting that this question or something very similar is still trekking around in Peter Hillary's mind to this day. A question like this can lead you down all kinds of soulful pathways of self-discovery. Of course, this is rarely a smooth ride but it does seem to be a trip worth taking.

I wanted to find out more about the kinds of questions people find useful to ask themselves in difficult times, so I decided to ask a group of people. Here is a sample of their favourites.

STEPHEN
- What am I feeling physically?
- How can I do this easier?
- What do I know at this point in my life?

JAN
- What is the most loving thing to do?
- Where is this taking me?
- What choices do I have?

SUE
- Is this what I need?
- Am I being true to myself?
- What is my deepest wish?
- How can I be my greatest for the world?

JIM
- What is it that's stressing me here?
- Which of the causes do I have any control over?
- Which ones can I act on right now?

DOUG
- What am I feeling right now?
- What am I leaving out?
- What's the key to this?

VINKA
- What's going on?
- Knowing what I know, how can I approach this challenge in my life?
- What can I learn from this?
- If I could live it over again, what would I do the same or differently?
- If everything was how I wanted it to be, what would it look like?

YOUR LIVING QUESTIONS

Can you think of any question(s) that you find particularly useful to ask yourself? Looking back over an experience of sadness that has now subsided, was there a question you found useful to ask yourself then? Is there a question you can think of now that would have been really useful to ask at that time? Is there a question from another time in your past that you found useful? Do any of the questions listed above catch your attention? List your 'living questions'.

Over the next few days, pay attention to the questions you hear, perhaps in a conversation, books, television programs, newspapers. Be on the lookout for questions that intrigue you;

> questions that seem to be significant for the wider context of your life. They may be curious questions, questions that fascinate, surprise, make you laugh, blow your mind or get to the nub of something. Add these questions to your list of living questions.
>
> Now choose one question from the list and turn it over in your mind for a day or so. Don't try to force an answer or solution, just let the question reverberate in your mind and see where it leads.

Sometimes a 'living question' prompts us to get down to the serious business of planning our life's trajectory. And sometimes it simply makes room for our imaginations to play and dream. Wild dreams, fantastical possibilities, exotic scenarios. The opportunity offered by the last phase in the cycle is to connect with what has been gathered during a time of sadness and to ask ourselves how we want to bring that forward into our daily lives. Our experience of soulful sadness has matured us as we have travelled with it through the cycle. Through the power of our attention, our soulful sadness has been refined and distilled into actions and ways of being that can enrich our lives. Hope has been generated by the soulful journey we have taken and we are invited to be the best we can be. This is our offering to ourselves and to the world.

Whether you use the energy of this last phase to plan how you will act on a huge life-altering decision, or simply to try something different, the question will ultimately boil down to this: What is my next simple step? Even if the problem or the situation which prompted your experience of soulful sadness remains big and the options huge, when you pull back into the next simple step, it all becomes more workable. As the thirty-second President of the United States, Franklin D. Roosevelt, once said: 'Above all, try something'.

What is my next simple step? This question goes to the heart of the cycle's purpose—to keep us flowing forward rather than freezing in fright and overwhelm. So we will leave the cycle with this one last reflection:

What is my next simple step?

CHAPTER 11

GO ON WITH YOUR STORY

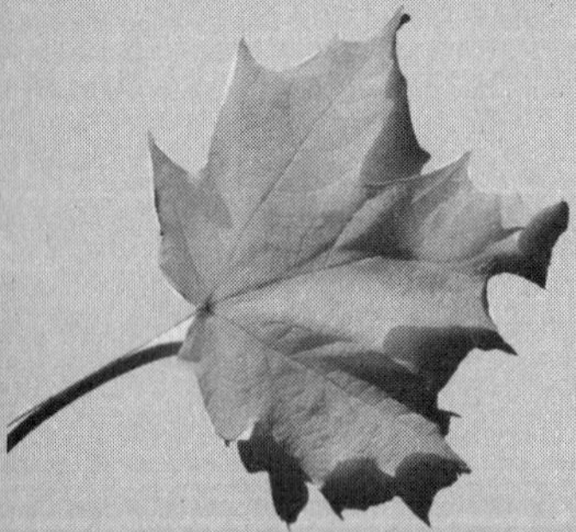

CHAPTER ELEVEN

The cycle of soulful sadness begins with the Call of the Soul and ends with the Call of the World. These two powerful and equally important calls set up a dynamic and never-ending interplay. With the call of the soul we are drawn on an arc inwards as we become aware of our longing for inner connection, stillness and solitude. With the call of the world, we are drawn on an arc outwards as we become aware of a pull towards outer connection, action and service.

Both are realms of great learning about connection and identity, and each gives meaning and balance to the other. A focus on one leads naturally to a focus on the other as we seek to know ourselves in the quiet of our being and then try to apply that knowledge in our interactions with others. Our 'story'—everything that happens in our life and how we interpret it—unfolds against the backdrop of these two equally soulful calls.

When I think of a human being holding and heeding both of these powerful calls, I am amazed—gobsmackingly amazed—by what a task this is. Our ongoing attempts to hold these two calls in balance creates an internal fire as we touch a point of balance only to slip and lose it again. No wonder we become confused and overheated at times—but what potential there is for expansion as well!

Feeling sad is a natural part of being human. Times of sadness do not necessarily mean something is going wrong. Rather, they can be potent times of transition, retreat and reflection; times to feel the longing of the heart, to reassess our goals and assumptions, and to hone our ability to be our own best friend. Rather than automatically labelling our everyday experiences of sadness as depression, we can become increasingly skilful at learning how to harvest the soulful gifts that are hidden within them—and we can share this practical skill with others, including the young people in our lives. Navigating sadness and difficulty is a lifelong task but young people may especially appreciate some clues about how to relate to their sad feelings at a time when they can be alarmingly buffeted by their highs and lows.

Because recoiling from sadness is the default setting in our society, it simply doesn't occur to most people to stop running away and to move closer to it. Even if we are intuitively aware that sadness carries gifts inherent within it, we may have no idea about *how* to be with our sadness. What might that look and feel like? What sorts of things might we be doing? How can we learn to transform our sadness? The value of the cycle of soulful sadness is that it offers suggestions for doing these things. Each phase in the cycle offers windows into the uses of sadness. By bringing your steady attention to sadness you will get to know the kinds of activities that serve you best as it unfolds and in this way you will learn how to befriend yourself when you need it most.

Your big-hearted attention to your experience will eventually open up ways for taking your discoveries forward into your life with renewed energy and enthusiasm. The idea is to follow the natural pull into each phase and take up the invitation to explore its unique flavour, trusting that you will be drawn into the next phase when the time is right.

Taking up the invitation to explore the unique flavour of each of the phases does not necessarily mean doing whatever you want. It means doing actions that are in tune with the flavour of that time; doing things that match the energy of the time in constructive and creative ways. This may be as simple as staying in for a peaceful night of pottering and reflection rather than going out to a noisy social event. Or it could mean coming up with playful activities that respect a radical impulse arising from within you. For example you may want to pack up the kids and move to Morocco right now. That may not be possible nor advisable. So instead of dismissing the thought as wayward or silly, you may decide to honour it in a small achievable way, such as cooking a meal with Moroccan spices. A yearning for the exotic can also be honoured and given space by buying a hot-pink scarf; the longing for something different can be satisfied by moving the furniture. This does not mean that there isn't a place for wholesale change, but it does help us honour the impulses that arise during a sad time in safe and playful ways, until the dust settles and we are ready to make decisions and plans.

Soulful melancholy, when entered into with respect and gentleness, eventually subsides and leads you back to engagement with life and community. Experiencing this builds trust and helps you make peace with sadness as one of the many flavours of a deeply rewarding life.

A soulful approach calls on you to keep opening your heart. Bringing soulfulness to an emotion or situation is not trying to force it in any one direction, not trying to suppress it or indulge it, but simply being with it and following the flow of it as it evolves. When you are prepared to cooperate with it as it shifts through its various forms, you will be softened by it.

The combination of your respectful attention mixed with the energy of the emotion itself opens the heart. Soulful sadness is not the ego having a tantrum; it is the soul coming to know itself. You begin to experience more of just being who you are without worrying too much about your own emotional overlays and judgements, and that's lovely. It is so satisfying, healthy and sane to be present and aware in each moment.

THE POWER OF ATTENTION—PATRICK

When I give my simple attention to what I would have previously called 'a depressed state', really be present to it and *with* it, neither prolonging it nor trying to make it go away, then it transforms and becomes soulful melancholy. It is the difference between being *with* myself and dropping the ball and running away from myself.

Once you become more familiar with the territory of sadness, you may find that you can relax a little more when sadness comes calling. As your view gets wider and more compassionate, the grip of sadness—the claw of it—loosens a little and you may not panic quite as much when sadness arises. Even if panic remains your first port of call, your knowledge of the territory will help you bring a healthy dose of recognition and wry humour to the mix, and this makes all the difference. In time, you may find yourself more inclined to 'rewrite' your stories of sadness and hard times with a greater sense of adventure and a cast of colourful characters.

However . . . and yet . . .

Time for a soulful pause: on some level sadness always undoes us. Each time we experience sadness it is real and true for us. While it is invaluable to get to know the territory of sadness and to realise that we have moved on before, and we will probably move on again, that doesn't mean we are numb or immune to the sting of sadness each time it comes calling.

The cycle will not help us tie sadness up in a neat little package. Becoming familiar with the cycle doesn't give us the lowdown on melancholy as if we had managed to catch a Beastie—preferably a Heffalump—and had him all corralled up in the back paddock, eating the grass and keeping the backyard nice and tidy. I have to confess right now, so no one is in any doubt, my backyard is sometimes very messy—the grass overgrown and the weeds rampant. The cycle is not a way to disarm sadness, make it predictable, or banish it to the nether regions. It is a way to enter into a living, breathing relationship with sadness, changing and flowing as it changes and flows. I hope it will offer you a way of bringing greater awareness and skill to the perennial human experience of melancholy.

Each time we go through a time of sadness there is an opportunity to refine our decisions about how we'll be and what we will do as the cycle takes place. Equally, each time we experience a time of sadness it is real for us; now is now and we are feeling it. Becoming familiar with the cycle of soulful melancholy is not a way to anaesthetise ourselves from feeling what humans feel. Even though we may have been through many cycles of soulful sadness, we never come to the next one with complete certainty. We can never control our experience of it, predict how it will go with unfailing accuracy, or even fully understand it with our Very Clever Brain. The cycle will not help us cobble together a neat little parcel called 'together person'. That will definitely unravel in a heap when sadness comes calling! We *will* feel and we will be a little undone each time we experience it, otherwise it would not be sadness—and being unmasked is part of the soulful power of it.

We may recognise soulful sadness takes us more fully into love, but each time we feel sadness coming on there may be a lingering uncertainty, a kernel of doubt: Does it really? Was I just imagining that love grows this way? Will I really find a way forward this time? That is why it is so tempting when sadness arises to wonder if you have made any progress at all. You may say, 'Oh, here I am yet again,' as you are hurt by something someone has said or disappointed in your own behaviour. Perhaps it is useful to think about our repeated journeys through soulful sadness as a spiral with many layers. Each loop in a spiral takes us past similar territory as the loop below, but in a different plane. We are subtly changed by each loop through sadness as we experience the impact on our body and soul, and as the meaning we give the experience shapes our ongoing 'story'.

Each time the descent of melancholy happens we can remind ourselves to take hold of the wisdom we have gathered from previous times about its deeper purpose, and yet the effort of bringing our attention to it—and opening to it—has to be refreshed each time. That effort might come down to doggedly holding your attention to a single beautiful thing, like the smell of honeysuckle as you brush past or the flash of light on water. But what a soulful and deeply satisfying effort that is. Perhaps the gathering of skill in walking alongside sadness is not really about making life easier but making it more exquisitely layered, faceted and coloured—and increasing our capacity to find the joy inherent in that.

Often it is not until the cycle is drawing to a close or even long after it has ended that we see what we have learnt and are then more inclined to value the experience. Insights do come—how delicious and what relief for a sad spirit—and yet it can take a long time for the wisdom contained in these insights to be fully imbibed. We grasp a truth and then promptly forget it. What we can understand intellectually often far outstrips what we are able to hold emotionally, and we may need to learn the same thing over and over before our whole self can stand present and accounted for in a new understanding. Our slowness in learning from repeated mistakes can itself be a source of soulful melancholy. Ah, what to do? Only a patient and compassionate heart will suffice.

Many of our experiences of sadness vanish, seemingly without trace. Thank goodness for this because we might not be able to bear such a weight of memory. Some of them we do remember vividly; they may have been particularly painful or we may have gathered an unforgettable lesson from them. But even these we cannot keep on a mantelpiece like trophies gathering dust. Their value is in what meaning we choose to extract from them and how they live in us now. All of our experiences, the forgotten ones as well as the remembered ones, are like water on stone—we may not see a trace of each wave but we do see the collective action of the tides. You can certainly feel it in a person when they have let their life experiences, both pleasant and sad, smooth their rough edges and keep on opening them even as those experiences of living and loving have also brought wrinkles to their faces.

WHAT RISES TO THE SURFACE—DANNY

I value hard times—but usually in retrospect! I do not like sad times or want them and would never consciously invite them. Hell no. No need, they come right in on their own. But I *have* learned to value them. I see that this is when I shake out of lethargy and really inquire, really seek, really learn. And something with light in it always rises to the surface, even when I think, this time it won't. But it always does.

As many people know only too well, sad times can be very dark and sometimes help is needed to find that chink of light. Anyone can get lost in a labyrinth of sadness, and an important skill in your sadness repertoire is recognising when you need help and knowing how to ask for it. If you feel stuck in a wasteland of sadness for a period of time that feels unhealthy for you, or if you sense that you are bogged in a horribly bleak place and that remaining there is no longer an opportunity to slowly gather what you are called upon to gather at this time, then please take the soulful action of seeking help. While soulful sadness is not a medical condition, depression is—and this does not mean that depression cannot also be a soulful experience. You can bring all your soulful attentiveness to an experience of depression, along with the medical assistance that might also be necessary for now. While not letting a superficial fear of sadness be the determining factor, there is deep wisdom in seeking professional advice when you know that you cannot access the resources you need at this time.

Sometimes sad events traumatise us to such an extent that we simply have to shut down for a time. There is no blame or shame in this. We know from our adventures in sad lands that letting something lie fallow is sometimes necessary. It can take the edge off the discomfort to realise that you are shutting down and tag it for attention later. Ultimately, things are nearly always workable because we can engage with them further down the track. Somehow the task is about allowing all of it—the shutting down and the opening up—to become grist for the mill in some way, even if a lot of time needs to go by before we can engage with it directly.

There aren't any hard-and-fast rules about how to navigate sadness. No one else can really judge what effort and skill is being applied by another, or where their breaking point is. The more you come to know yourself as you travel within the spectrum of sadness, the more you will trust your own judgement about what is healthy and life-giving for you at any particular time.

While recoiling from sadness is not the answer, neither is holding on to it for too long. The essence of any cycle is movement, and the idea of taking up the valuable opportunities that sadness offers is so that we can allow sadness to move and transform. In some soulfully incomprehensible way, we embrace sadness so that we can let it go. In this way, learning to digest sadness is a fundamental part of learning how to be happy. Respecting and valuing sadness doesn't mean grasping it tightly to us and creating an identity out of it. We have all met people who seem to be doing this or we may be doing it ourselves; somehow being sad has become who we are and we wear our sadness like an identity bracelet. Who would we be if we were not permanently downcast or indulging in some sad drama? Soulful sadness requires a much bigger embrace than that.

Some experiences of grief, such as the death of a loved one, may never leave us—and we would not want them to because they are seared into our very soul; to be rid of them would be to cut a deep gouge out of our own being. While grief like this may never lose its unfathomable pain, it does subtly change and can eventually be experienced as part of the precious love we have for lost ones. It takes one heck of a huge heart to bear this, and it is just so extraordinarily humbling to realise that so many people live this out on a daily basis. This is not what I mean when I caution about creating an identity out of sadness. I am speaking about the ways in which a downtrodden gloom can become a habit, an endless loop held in place by the way we speak to ourselves and others, by our posture, by the food we eat, by the way we make our own superficial desires central to everything, by our unexamined values and actions, by our fear of reaching for happiness.

Our attitude throughout the cycle needs to be focused and present, honest and real, yet also soft and flowing. We do need to be willing for the cycle to lead us into dark and dingy corners, but also for it to lead us back out into service and engagement with the world again, even if the way we choose to do that is significantly changed by our sad time.

The value of being present and conscious while you are experiencing sadness is so that you can step into what you learn; wearing it, owning it, inhabiting it so that it builds your resilience and is accessible from then on. While everyday sadness can unravel you, you can decide not to be ripped to shreds by it. It is good if the core of you remains intact and gathers a little something each time. The only force I know that can keep the soul intact and growing in the face of everything a human may face, or heal it after a shattering breach, is love. In the end, even in the presence of excruciating sadness, we have to reach inside and somehow take hold of the willingness to love. That's what it comes down to.

While that sounds like serious business, when it come to sadness, a light touch is a welcome skill. Sometimes it might even be time to take a leaf out of St Thomas Aquinas' book; he said that sorrow can be alleviated by a good sleep, a bath and a glass of wine. Definitely worth a try! Whatever activities we choose, we do very well to practise carrying sadness as lightly as possible.

I once had a dream in which someone said, 'Love is a feather.' I woke up with this phrase resonating in my mind. I knew it was a gift that contained a key and that it was important to unlock its significance.

Love is a feather. Such a simple sentence but what does it mean? I puzzled about this for quite a while. In my mind's eye I could see a soft downy white feather on the palm of a hand. I thought about the beauty and lightness of a feather. How it almost floats; how the open palm barely feels the weight of the feather and yet delights in its delicate softness.

Over time this image has come to symbolise for me the kind of effort that is required to digest sadness and hold a state of love. The effort has to be full but not weighty. The experience has to be held lightly on an open palm. Love and happiness can be crushed when you try to grasp them too hard.

Some extraordinary human beings show us that sadness can be held as if it were a feather on the palm, and not a heavy burden weighing them down or a ratty pile of rocks in a sack dragging behind them. I am reminded of Nelson Mandela, the Dalai Lama or Mother Teresa, or myriad everyday, anonymous people who may have every reason to feel burdened by the suffering and sadness they have witnessed but instead find every reason to love anyway.

It is useful to find an image (such as a feather on a palm) that can symbolise an important piece of wisdom about sadness for you. A symbol is an effective way of carrying forward what you have learnt and making it easily accessible. The image needs to be captivating and meaningful to you. As you know, sometimes an insight or series of thoughts hits you like a ton of bricks, but then later, like a dream sequence you think you will never forget, you can't quite grasp the insight anymore. How does it go again? You forget what comes first and what comes next. But a symbol gathers potency around it and is easily recalled, especially if it has arisen spontaneously. Like a dream, a symbol has its own language, perhaps the language of the soul. At first the meaning of the image may be quite mysterious and you may need to contemplate it for a while. But once you have begun to penetrate it, then the message of the symbol becomes something that you can access immediately without needing to go via the intellect or words.

> **FINDING SYMBOLS**
>
> Is there an image that can symbolise an important understanding or insight about soulful sadness for you? It may be something intriguing that you heard or saw. It may be something that occurred in a dream, or an image from a book, greeting card, photograph, painting or movie. Or it may be a scene from your daily life that caught your attention such as a baby grasping a finger, a person sitting quietly under a tree, a colourful umbrella, a beautiful cake, waves rolling in and out on a beach. Or it may be a universal symbol that appeals to you right now, such as a circle, a labyrinth, a dove, an iceberg. Don't struggle to find a symbol if it is not arising easefully. If an image does present itself then take hold of it, gently reflect on its meaning and recall it in moments when you wish to access its message.

In a busy life our mental space can become crowded and chaotic. This causes distress and overload, and a period of sadness can be the prompt we need to slow down and take some time out. The seven-phase cycle of soulful sadness—feeling the pull of longing, sitting in not knowing, becoming receptive, allowing an encounter with upliftment, embracing ambiguity, and then taking up the challenge of working out priorities and plans for the best actions we can muster . . . this cycle calls for stillness and reflection. This period of retreat opens up a nurturing space within and gives us time to find the images, music, poetry and gestures that describe our experience, rather than solve it.

This book is based on a simple assertion—that it is of great value to turn our attention within ourselves. Our own attention has great power. How does sadness transform? Through our attention and presence. Most of the time when an emotion arises, our energy and attention is taken up in trying to prolong it if it is pleasant or make it go away if it is not. We rarely stop to simply be with it, to gaze at it, to open and soften enough to simply be present with it.

The world's spiritual giants have always said that silence and solitude play a vital role in gathering the capacity to give our attention in a simple and unwavering way. This leads, they tell us, to the uncovering of deep Happiness, which has earned that capital 'H'. This Happiness is not an emotion and it is not the opposite of sadness. This deep Happiness is not affected by the comings and goings of sad events, boring things, moods arising and subsiding, stuff happening. And just like our word 'sad', one word cannot communicate all the nuances of this Happiness—other words such as Satisfaction, Contentment, Wellbeing and Peace are also required; and they all need capitals when referring to the enormity of the state that arises when a person truly understands that the core of their being is not sad, and that feeling sad is no reason not to be happy.

There is a force within that propels us to seek insight, understanding and wisdom. There is a movement from within us towards transformation and breakthrough. It is as natural as breathing. This force takes each of us on a journey of learning and self-discovery. It is the same impetus that makes a seed sprout and form a little shoot; that makes a child want to explore and grow up and yearn to become more fully itself. It is life living itself through you.

Sadness is a potent agent for this force for growth.

When we refuse to accept any mood other than a superficial 'everything's perfectly okay and see me smile' because we have made sadness wrong and even shameful, then we do not allow ourselves access to the deepening power of soulful sadness, and a dry, brittle depression or a serious addiction can easily be the result. Soulful sadness is part of creating a deeper emotional intelligence; it is one of the flavours to cook with, to grow with.

It seems to me that imbedded within every experience, no matter how wonderful, is a kind of longing that acts as a subtle counterpoint. Because we do not understand the value of longing in our culture, we often mistake it for sadness or even depression. We don't know, as some other cultures do, that longing is not the same as desire or craving and that it is in fact a precious thing. Longing is an invitation to come back to centre; it is a yearning for balance and stillness—a yearning for our true home.

Soulful sadness is not a medical condition. It is not an illness; it is an ache, a longing. It is deep and full and can be very mournful, but it doesn't feel sorry for itself or call attention to itself through a downtrodden misery. It is actually full of love. Through it we can come into relationship with our own being. It is a prayerful space, it is a deep listening. It is difficult to reflect with true sincerity when we are constricted with ego, focused with trying to present an image or impress, but in soulful melancholy the ego lets go for a time and we can mature in silence. And, paradoxically, an accumulation of sad times can be the momentum we need to step into a passionate embrace of happiness.

THE BEST REVENGE—AXEL

I am a social worker and the thing that keeps me going is something a woman who has lived a lifetime of trauma and abuse said to me two years ago. She said, 'After everything I have been through, I have decided the best revenge is to live a happy life.' I am humbled and inspired by this.

If your sadness is really weighing you down and you feel that you have lost the capacity to let it help you grow, try spending some time around people who have suffered a great deal and yet have still found their way to joy. Or alternatively, try spending some time around children. Children's points of view are often so fresh and light that they delight and challenge our accepted ideas of how things are. Their state of wonder is infectious and they invite us to look at things in a new and magical way.

THE MEANING OF WASTE—ANITA

I had been feeling inexplicably sad for quite a while. And then one morning I had a delightful moment with my four-year-old daughter that somehow helped me slip out of my blues. She turned to me and said, 'Mummy, I know what the word *waste* means.'

'Do you, darling?' I asked.

'Yes,' she said. 'It's when you run the water in the tap and don't use it.' I see the pleased look on her face. I can almost hear the wheels of her mind thinking, 'Yes, rather good, I've really nailed that.'

Then a frown appears on her face and suddenly everything is not so sure anymore. 'But if you have some stairs in your house and you don't walk up them, is that a waste too?' she asks.

I seriously consider it for a moment. Then my brain comes to a complete halt. The neurons misfire. It does not compute. I burst out laughing.

Some people say, 'I love being with children because they keep me young.' Children bring the suppleness, freshness and optimism that characterise growth. In the same way we must remain 'young' and supple with our sadness. If you become rigid, bad-tempered, pessimistic and exhausted then it's hard to let your sadness bring you gifts. But if you can stay flexible and fluid while experiencing sadness, these times will bring surprising insights and unexpected outcomes.

I wonder what can help us most to find this fluidity and flexibility as we respond to the rise and fall of the emotions, including sadness? Perhaps it is something that we all have; something so simple and so fundamental that we may never have given it a thought. Perhaps it is the breath—that ever-present in–out flow that bridges the Call of the World and the Call of the Soul. It is not surprising that the breath is the focus of so many therapies, ranging from releasing anxiety and working with addiction all the way to entering the deepest states of meditation. The in-breath: pulling our gaze to the extraordinary internal landscape as it travels in and suffuses the body; the out-breath: emerging from the body and inviting our gaze out to the fantastical array of external things. Any activities that promote the natural, steady rhythm of the breath will be supportive during sad times.

In all likelihood you will go on having experiences of sadness, times of disappointment and confusion, flashes of longing. And over and over you can choose to engage with them consciously and soulfully, eventually and always finding your way back to one hugely courageous question, 'Even from here, can I open my heart?'

Through transforming your vision and experience of sadness you can learn a great deal about the art of creating happiness. You probably won't come out of sad times rubbing your hands together and thinking, 'Well, great! Now I've got sadness all sorted.' Instead, you may stand there—perhaps a bit dishevelled, perhaps with another wrinkle and a few more grey hairs—but very likely gazing in amazement at the immensity of it all. Wherever you find yourself, you can open your arms and love from there. You can go on with your story.

APPENDIX

Here is a copy of the seven phases in the cycle of soulful sadness for easy reference

CYCLE OF SOULFUL SADNESS

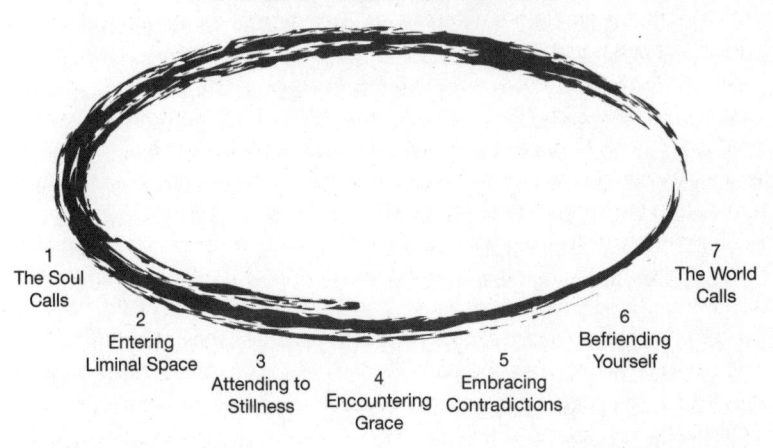

1. The Soul Calls
2. Entering Liminal Space
3. Attending to Stillness
4. Encountering Grace
5. Embracing Contradictions
6. Befriending Yourself
7. The World Calls

1 THE SOUL CALLS—LONGING

Somehow, nothing has quite turned out the way I expected. I have tried really hard, given it my best shot, but somehow, even the good things seem tinged with disappointment. It's time to let go of rushing around and to be still. Something's calling me from within. I am yearning for something. I am longing for something. I am homesick. Even though I am at home, still I am yearning for my true home. I see and hear that longing everywhere: I think of soulful calls—like the call of a whale, the mournful sound of a single tuba, and a ship's foghorn in the mist. Images like an eagle circling on the thermals. It's time to pause and be alone.

The soul is calling me.

2 ENTERING LIMINAL SPACE—NOT KNOWING

I have to admit, I have no answers. I truly don't know what move to make next, what decision to make. I sigh. I let go. I just don't know. I am in between. Suspended. I don't know the way forward, the way back, or even how I got here. I might even say, 'I give up', 'What's the point?' and 'Is change really possible?' I don't know if it will all work out or not. I can't pretend. The old answers no longer seem to hold water. There aren't any new ones to put in their place either. I have to sit in not knowing, and wait. I gently simmer in this. Endurance. Courage. The long note.

The truth is, I just don't know.

3 ATTENDING TO STILLNESS—DEEP LISTENING

As I accept not knowing and simply wait, I begin to listen beyond my own thoughts and feelings. I notice the throb of my blood in my ears. I hear my breath coming in and going out. I fall into the sounds of silence. The creaking of the house, the sound of traffic in the distance. I fall into quiet daydreams in random places. I linger in the car after parking it. I read poetry, write in my journal, listen to music, stare at the fire, say a prayer. I am slow to return phone calls. I am in retreat. The more I listen, the stiller I become, and somehow the longing begins to sweeten. My own pat answers have fallen away and I want to attend more carefully to each moment. I am a little more humble and I begin to open to the possibility that I can learn. I begin to really listen to people when they talk, notice signs, attend to stillness.

I become still enough to truly listen.

4 ENCOUNTERING GRACE—THE TURNING POINT

As I arrive more fully in the present moment, I notice that it's okay. More than okay—it's actually benevolent. Suddenly, I encounter a 'happening', a moment of beauty, a sight that moves me, a thought that uplifts me and fills my heart. A red balloon floating away in the blue sky, a genuine smile on someone's face, a dog wagging its entire back end in welcome, something someone says, a flash of insight, the sight of someone really trying, a numberplate with an unexpected message, the way the curtain wafts. Perhaps for the tiniest moment, I encounter something sacred. For a time, even a second or two, my mind stops in its tracks and is amazed. Gravity releases me. I let go. I am effortlessly supported. What a relief. I drink in this life-giving nourishment. In the afterglow of that encounter what I say and do is perfectly in tune. My whole being is watered, softened and expanded.

I am moved and nothing is quite the same.

5 EMBRACING CONTRADICTIONS—HOLDING THE OPPOSITES

Touched by that encounter, my mind can bring me treasures now. I see with compassionate eyes. I see that most of the time we are all trying our best. Things are far more layered than I thought. For now, I am able to let go of control and perfection, and I am released from my own harsh judgement. I have stopped thinking in terms of black or white, right or wrong, good or bad. I see that beauty and sadness are forever mixed. Love and hate, happiness and sadness, pleasure and pain, and all the opposites are always at play. Each is an aspect of the other. I can feel them all at the same time. I am both happy and sad . . . and all is well. This is the way it is.

I am big enough to hold the opposites.

6 BEFRIENDING YOURSELF—MAKING CONSCIOUS CHOICES

Even though I can see that everything has a place at the table and there are endless possibilities, I cannot choose them all. Some things will serve and some will not. I must apply a discerning eye. I stand back now and take stock of what is important to me. Each of my actions has consequences and I want to choose wisely and gather my will. I identify my cherished values. I review my actions and habits. I assess which actions are truly authentic for me, and which ones aren't. Which ones reflect my values and make my heart sing? I know ultimately it is up to me to make my life meaningful. I view all this with soft and loving eyes, knowing that I will sometimes stumble. I speak kindly to myself and am my own best friend.

I am responsible for the choices and meaning in my life.

7 THE WORLD CALLS—OFFERING

With greater clarity I walk forward and engage with my world. I greet the moment with a renewed sense of hope and optimism. Many possibilities and ideas are emerging and I make plans to implement them skilfully. I relish questions and spark creatively with others. My actions are conscious and bright. I have something to offer and I look forward to making a contribution. I consider my life's purpose and sharpen my intention. I welcome my own leadership and the leadership of others. I feel courageous, energetic and centred. I am ready to participate, engage and offer my service generously.

The world is calling me.

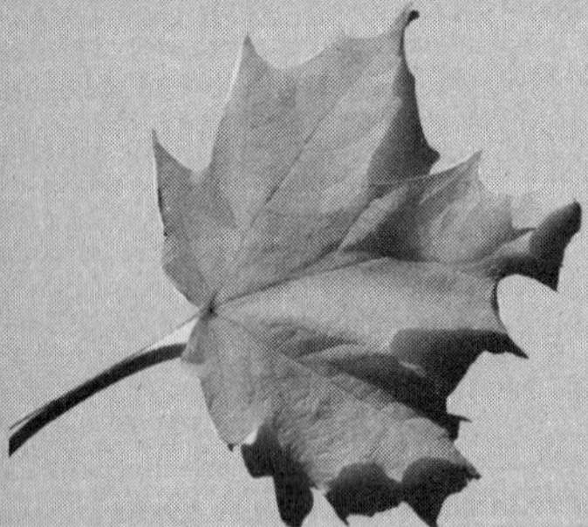

REFERENCES AND FURTHER READING

Franz Kafka, quoted in Ian Baker, *The Heart of the World*, The Penguin Press, New York, 2004.

Jane Bennett, *A Blessing Not a Curse*, Sally Milner Publishing, Bowral, 2002.

Jane Benett and Alexandra Pope, *The Pill: Are You Sure It's For You?* Allen & Unwin, Sydney, 2008.

John B. Carroll (ed.), *Language, Thought and Reality: Selected Writings of Benjamin Lee Whorf*, MIT Press, Boston, 1956.

Jag Parvesh Chander (ed.), *Teachings of Mahatma Gandhi*, The Indian Printing Works, Lahore [date not shown].

Pema Chödrön, *When Things Fall Apart*, Element, HarperCollins, London, 2003.

Piero Ferrucci, *Inevitable Grace*, Jeremy P. Tarcher/Putnam Books, New York, 1990.

Michael J. Gelb, *How to Think Like Leonardo da Vinci: Seven Steps to Genius Every Day*, Dell Publishing, New York, 2000.

Natalie Goldberg, *The Long Quiet Highway: Waking Up in America*, Bantam Books, New York, 1993.

Matsuo Basho, quoted in Robert Hass, *The Essential Haiku: Versions of Basho, Buson and Issa*, Ecco/HarperCollins, New York, 1994.

James Hillman, *The Soul's Code: In Search of Character and Calling*, Random House, New York, 1996.

Roger Housden, *Ten Poems to Change your life*, Hodder & Stroughton, London, 2002.

—— *Ten Poems to Open Your Heart*, Hodder & Stoughton, London, 2003.

Abbott Christopher Jamison, *Finding Sanctuary: Monastic Steps for Everyday Life*, Weidenfeld and Nicolson, London, 2006.

Matthew Johnstone, *I Had A Black Dog*, Pan, Sydney, 2005.

Jeffrey Kacirk, *The Word Museum*, Touchstone, Simon & Schuster, New York, 2000.

Jack Kornfield, *After the Ecstasy, the Laundry*, Random House, London, 2000.

Elisabeth Kübler-Ross, *On Death and Dying*, Touchstone, Simon & Schuster, New York, 1969.

Daniel Ladinsky, *The Subject Tonight is Love: 60 Wild and Sweet Poems*, Pumpkin House Press, South Carolina, 2000,

Michael Leunig, *When I Talk to You: A Cartoonist Talks to God*, HarperCollins, Sydney, 2004.

Eric Maisel, *Deep Writing: 7 Principles that Bring Ideas to Life*, Tarcher/Putnam, New York, 1999.

—— *The Van Gogh Blues: The Creative Person's Path Through Depression*, Rodale, Emmaus, 2002.

Gerald G. May, *The Dark Night of the Soul*, HarperCollins, New York, 2004.

Thomas Moore, *Soul Mates: Honoring the Mysteries of Love and Relationship*, HarperCollins, New York, 1994.

—— *The Soul of Sex: Cultivating Life as an Act of Love*, HarperCollins, New York, 1998.

Peter O'Connor, *Looking Inwards*, Penguin Books, Melbourne, 2003.

Albert Rothenberg, 'Janusian Thinking and Creativity', *The Psychoanalytic Study of Society VII*, 1976, pp. 1–30, appearing in *The Psychoanalytic Quarterly*, vol. 49, 1980.

John Tarrant, *The Light Inside the Dark: Zen, Soul, and the Spiritual Life*, HarperCollins, New York, 1998.

Chogyam Trungpa, *The Myth of Freedom and the Way of Meditation*, Shambhala Publications, Boston, 2002.

Stuart Walton, *Humanity: An Emotional History*, Atlantic Books, London, 2004.